Children
in Play Therapy

CLARK MOUSTAKAS, Ph.D.

JASON ARONSON, INC., PUBLISHERS

For Betty Moustakas
Like the little prince
Seeing rightly with the heart
What is essential
What is invisible to the eye

Library of Congress Catalog Card Number: 73-81216
ISBN: 0-87668-102-X

Manufactured in the United States of America

Preface

Returning to *Children in Play Therapy* was for me like a return to a deep, significant place of the past. Voices from those early struggles with children and families reawakened in me and created profoundly moving experiences. Images kept reappearing and once again, in a clear and vivid sense, I was in touch with faces and sounds, and expressions, and signs of the growing freedom of children as they emerged from dead and frightening scenes to new awareness and new life. Each child became clearly identified and present before me. We were sharing again that private world where two people may live fully behind closed doors without fear of judgment, surveillance or retaliation. In each instance, the process was recreated and I could see once more the unfolding journey of the child engaged in imaginative play and in a dialogue that represented natural means of coming alive again and restoring a sense of self.

Sometimes in rereading the transcriptions of conversation I winced at the awkwardness of my language, sometimes at my slowness to perceive and put into action important insights, yet at the heart of each meeting were basic attitudes of faith in the child's potential for finding a healthy way, acceptance of the child's words and actions, and respect for the child's style, peculiarity, and form of expressing and being. In any case, my slow and occasionally repetitive or unsteady commentary, did not impede the child's movement forward in learning to be free and in creating more effective means of relating and communicating. Thus, the essentials in value were all there—a desire to live deeply, genuinely, a desire to facilitate, and a belief in the powers of two people to create and enrich and grow together.

It is strange to think that the children in this book are now grown adults. A few of them I occasionally meet and within me I experience a special kind of joy, having participated in their lives at a time of crisis and having witnessed a renewal of themselves and their relations with others. Beyond this, between us even now there is an openness and a freedom to share and a unique and special kind of intimacy. Recently, a graduate student at the University of Illinois approached me and in a sudden rush of feeling embraced me warmly and fully. I had not seen him for almost twenty years yet he vividly remembered our meetings in play therapy when he was enrolled in the Merrill-Palmer Nursery School. Arm in arm we walked around the campus sharing those special moments of the past. To my surprise, he recalled many of the significant episodes in play and for awhile only the two of us existed in the mass of rushing people.

When I was first approached about the reprinting of this book, I doubted that what I had written twenty years ago could still be of value yet in the reading I found myself absorbed in a here and now sense. I found myself affirming the values and the nature of the process of play therapy—though not in each instance the specific words I used. I have concluded following the current return, that *Children in Play Therapy* still speaks to those concerned with fear and anger, with conflict and pain, with rejection and denial, with frozen and broken moments in relationships, with struggles of will and control, with efforts to know children's feelings and to reach a depth of expression and release. I believe the transactions of child and therapist in these pages remain guidelines for parents and teachers and for therapists seeking to develop healthy patterns of listening and of being sensitively alive with children—if not in the words then in the attitudes and values and in the spirit of what it ultimately means to take a journey down with another human being and then to see that person rise again.

In a few critical instances I have made changes in the language in order to bring the book into my present modes of thought and vocabulary.

CLARK MOUSTAKAS

April, 1973
Detroit, Michigan

CAROL'S SONG:
   Nobody knows what I know.
   Nobody knows what I know.
   Nobody goes where I go.
   Nobody wants to go where I go.
   Nobody wants to go where I go
   You take the dirt, and you take
      the water, and you mix it together.
   Water and sand.
   Rub it, squeeze it, mix it.
   That's what you do in here.
   You mix things the way you want.
   I'm gonna make some pie, I am.
   And then there won't be any more time.
   I'm gonna make a pie so big it's
      gonna cover the whole place up.
   The biggest pie you ever saw.
   There's my pie.
   And now I'm gonna cut it up in little
      pieces and share it with all the
      people.

Contents

CHAPTER I

Attitudes and Process of Play Therapy

Play therapy is a relatively new psychological field of human endeavor. There are a variety of approaches which have been found effective, particularly with disturbed children. These approaches differ in their philosophies and in their theories of personality dynamics (12).* They are similar in that they contain human values which the therapist attempts to communicate. Techniques, tools, and methods play a large role in therapy. But the particular values of the therapist pervade the relationship and, to a large degree, determine its therapeutic effectiveness. What the therapist says and does is important. How he feels is even more important. The feeling tones behind the therapist's statements and actions are of the greatest significance.

Client-centered therapists (5, 18) working with both children and adults differentiate more clearly than any other approach the basic philosophy presented in this volume. Child-centered play therapy is a relatively new approach. It has been used tentatively in a variety of ways. It has been used with some definite success with emotionally disturbed children, with children diagnosed as feeble-minded and physically handicapped children, with children

* Parenthetical numbers refer to numbered items in the References section at the end of the book.

1

retarded in reading and other school subjects, with children having situational problems, and with normal children. All these applications have been attempts to help teachers, parents, and their children to have more accurate understanding of each other and to learn to express their feelings more spontaneously and clearly and at the same time within some degree of control.

Unfortunately, too much stress in "nondirective" writings has been given to the skill of responding, skill in what to say. Actually, reflection of feelings, the major client-centered "technique," may easily be perceived as a repetitious, unsympathetic, static response. It may not lead either to emotional or intellectual insight, and, used superficially, reflections often stop real exploration of attitudes. The major function of reflection of feelings should be to convey through empathy the values or attitudes that the therapist believes an integral part of therapy, in the hope that it will lead to emotional clarification.

The child-centered philosophy is thus not mainly concerned with techniques and skills but rather with the kind of relationship which enables children to grow emotionally and to gain faith in themselves as feeling individuals. Emphasis here will be on how the normal child as well as the disturbed child may use play therapy as a growth experience.

THE ATTITUDES

Play therapy may be thought of as a set of attitudes in and through which children may feel free enough to express themselves fully, in their own way, so that eventually they may achieve feelings of security, adequacy, and worthiness through emotional insight. The belief is that these attitudes are communicable. They can be transmitted from one person to another. They cannot be taught, but they can be learned.

The three basic attitudes in child-centered play therapy are faith, acceptance, and respect. There is no clear-cut formula by which the therapist conveys these attitudes, since they blend imperceptibly in interpersonal relations. Faith is an intangible quality. It is something which is known largely through feelings, not through intellectualizations, and it is essential to emotional organization and growth. As yet we do not know when or how the process of faith evolves and is transmitted from one person to another. We are certain only that in the presence of another person who has faith in us, we somehow grasp that feeling and are able to face ourselves, to grow within ourselves, and to create more of ourselves so that we operate in terms of the people we really are.

Faith is expressed between the therapist and the child in both subtle and direct ways. The child becomes aware of the feelings the therapist has toward him. He senses whether this other person has faith in him. Children have described this feeling of faith as the most important quality in their play experiences: *

. . . you were the first person who ever believed in me—who didn't think I was all bad—who didn't think I was silly—who took the time to try to find out how I felt about things.

I think this all happened to me because you gave me a chance to believe in *me*. And then I felt I *was* worth while. . . . As I think back about it you didn't seem to do a thing but *be* there. And yet a harbor doesn't do anything either, except to stand there quietly with arms always outstretched waiting for the travelers to come home. I came home to myself through you.

I guess I found out that I could be what I wanted to be and how I felt was more important than how I looked. I couldn't do that though until I believed it myself by the way I felt.

And the feeling I got before I was through—a feeling that meant a lot to me—a feeling that to you and to me I made sense and I was a person worth while.

Faith is reflected in the child when he considers himself to be an important person, someone who has something to offer to himself and others. The child who has faith in himself believes in himself. He has convictions which are an integral part of him. He makes decisions for himself and carries them out. He expresses himself freely and fully and does not fear that he will be condemned for his feelings or his beliefs. The child who feels faith knows what he

* Appreciation is expressed to Laurance Shaffer, editor, and Virginia Axline, author, for permission to use these excerpts from "Play Therapy Experiences as Described by Child Participants," *J. Consult. Psychol.*, 1950, 14(1), 53–63.

wants to do, what he can do, and what he will do. He trusts his own feelings.

The therapist who has faith in the child sometimes conveys this faith in simple expressions. "That's up to you," "You're the best judge of that," or "The important thing is that you do what you want to do" are often used. However, these are mere words in themselves. The same words could express disbelief or sarcasm. To have therapeutic meaning, they must stem from a real attitude of faith, an expression of the therapist's deep belief that children have within themselves capacity for self-growth and self-realization.

Acceptance is a less elusive quality than faith. It is more clearly differentiated and better understood. Acceptance is not mere acquiescence. It is not a passive process, nor is it a noncommittal attitude. It implies a real commitment on the part of the therapist, a feeling that must be made known to the child. It involves real activity between the child and the therapist, and it is in this interaction alone that the child can feel accepted. Acceptance implies that the therapist actively accepts the child's feelings and his personal meanings, his perceptions.

To different children, objects have different meanings. In children's imaginations sand, clay, water, and the like may symbolize almost anything—a parent, a sibling, a painful experience, fears, food, love and hate, hostility. These fantasies are accepted by the therapist. Children are encouraged to explore their feelings further through such media. Objects with more definite structure, such as cars, knives, soldiers, guns, and boats, also may symbolize many things to children. The therapist accepts the child's symbolism exactly as it is and does not in any way try to enforce society's labels in children's play.

The play therapist may verbally indicate acceptance by many expressions: "Mm-hm," "I see," "That's the way you feel," "You're really afraid of him," "It can be anything you want it to be," "What do you see it as?" It should be remembered that it is not only through the words themselves that the child feels accepted, but through the feelings of the therapist who expresses them. Acceptance is shown throughout the whole relationship. The therapist may say nothing. He still conveys an attitude of acceptance if he feels along with the child.

A feeling of acceptance is threatened if the therapist in any way criticizes or disapproves, or if he rewards and approves. A child who is rewarded or approved may tend to limit himself to those actions and expressions which bring favor. He will not accept many of his own inner feelings that are in conflict or that are opposed to the approved feelings. Criticism produces similar results. Thus both approval and disapproval appear to hinder the therapeutic process, so it is important for the play therapist to be completely accepting at all times.

Closely allied to faith and acceptance is the attitude of respect. A child who feels respected feels that his interests and his feelings are understood. He feels that the therapist is concerned about him as a person. He realizes, too, that the therapist really shows consideration for him and wants to help him to help himself. The therapist who conveys respect does so in the way he greets the child, in the way he empathetically follows the child in his play, and in the way he shows the child that he understands his feelings. All these contribute to successful therapy.

The therapist respects the child for who he is at that time, at that moment, not for who he should be or who he might become. The therapist might say, in effect, to the child: "These are your feelings and you have the right to feel them. I shall not try to take them away from you, to divert you from them, or to deny them to you, for they are a part of you, and I shall honor them as I do all aspects of your self."

An adolescent girl clearly reveals this attitude of respect in her relationship with the therapist: *

. . . and you never dug into me like I was a person without feelings. You let me have my own world my own way and did not try to snatch it away from me . . . it was as though you said to me you can hate and you can be sad and you can feel cheated by your mother because that

* Appreciation is expressed to Laurance Shaffer, editor, and Virginia Axline, author, for permission to use this excerpt from "Play Therapy Experiences as Described by Child Participants," *J. Consult. Psychol.,* 1950 14(1), 53–63.

was the way I felt, and so I didn't have to lie to you or feel ashamed because I was me. . . .

The therapist respects the child by following him and attempting to see him as he is, at his own level. He respects the child's habits and mannerisms as part of his personality. He does not attempt to force the child or persuade him to modify his standards so that they are in agreement with those of the therapist or any other individual or group in society. The therapist who respects the child sees the child as a person who has ever-present potentialities for helping himself.

Respect, then, goes one step beyond acceptance. The attitude of respect considers all feelings and attitudes, all ways and values that a child reveals and that have been accepted by the therapist as facets of the child's personality which in and of themselves have unique worth for the child at that time.

Faith, acceptance, and respect are thus seen as intimately bound in the therapeutic relationship. Faith is the most pervasive attitude, a belief in the child's potentials for working out his difficulties and for discovering what is best for him in his reality. Acceptance and respect are more specific in nature. The accepting play therapist encourages the child to express his feelings and himself fully and to explore his attitudes more thoroughly. Respect in the relationship indicates to the child that his self is regarded as worth while and important.

The play therapist should examine himself in his relationship with the child not only in terms of the techniques and tools that he employs in each session, but also in terms of whether or not he is conveying faith, acceptance, and respect, where and how in each play therapy session he has succeeded, and where and how he has failed to achieve these goals. Without these basic attitudes in the social-emotional climate of play therapy, it would be difficult to imagine effective therapy of any kind.

THE THERAPEUTIC PROCESS

The therapeutic process itself seems to follow a regular pattern. It is perhaps clearly observable with disturbed children. However, certain aspects of the process are evident in therapy sessions with normal children too, usually in milder form and of shorter duration.

The picture seems to be as follows: The emotions of disturbed children and troubled children to a large degree, at the beginning of therapy, are diffuse and undifferentiated. The feelings are generally negative. Children have apparently lost contact with the people and the situations that originally aroused frustration, anger, fear, and guilt. Their emotions, in other words, are no longer tied to reality. They are magnified, generalized, and easily stimulated and evoked.

Attitudes of hostility, anxiety, and regression are pervasive in their expression in the playroom. Children are frightened, angry, or immature without definitely focusing their feelings on any particular person or persons or emotional experiences. They are often afraid of almost everything and everybody and sometimes feel like destroying all people, or merely wish they would be left completely alone, or wish to regress to a simpler, less demanding level of behavior. The basic attitudes of anxiety and hostility in the child motivating his behavior are used here to illustrate the process. Anger, for example, may express itself by direct attacks on the toys, by smashing, pounding, breaking, by tearing, crushing and a variety of other actions. These attacks seem to be without purpose. Apparently, there is nothing in the therapy situation which provokes them. The child is left free with his own impulses, and the level of the relationship with the therapist to a great degree determines the amount and quality of the hostility expressed. The greater the child's trust in the therapist and the greater his feeling of acceptance and respect, the more focused his anger may be.

As the relationship between the child and the therapist is clarified and strengthened, the attitude of hostility becomes gradually sharpened and more specific. Anger now is expressed more directly and often is related to particular persons or experiences. Pounding and smashing, even the expression of the desire to kill, may still be present, but in this second stage of the therapeutic process it is a parent, or a sibling, or perhaps the entire family that is attacked. The therapist or any other person may be attacked or denounced or threatened in the child's play. As the child expresses and releases more and more of these negative feelings in direct ways toward the people in his life who aroused them and made him feel inadequate, and as these expressions are accepted by the therapist, the feelings become less intense and affect the child less in his total experiences. The child begins to feel that he is a worthy person.

A third level of the process now begins to appear. The child is no longer so completely negative in his expressions of feelings. Anger is still specific, but he shows a variety of ambivalences toward particular people in his life. For example, the child's anger toward his baby brother or sister may fluctuate in his play between feeding and caring for the baby and spanking the baby or mistreating him in other ways. These ambivalent reactions may be severe in intensity at first, but as they are expressed again and again in the therapeutic relationship, they become less tense. In the final stage of this process, positive feelings begin to emerge. The child now sees himself and his relationships with people more as they really are. He may still resent the baby, but he no longer hates the baby merely because he is the baby. As a four-year-old once put it in one of her final sessions, "I'm going to have a big party and invite everybody, even my baby brother." The process of anger may be summarized in these four stages. First, it appears diffuse and pervasive. Next, it becomes focused in the form of hostility toward parents, siblings, other children, the therapist, relatives, or other people in the child's life. Third, anger remains specific and becomes mixed with positive attitudes not yet completely differentiated. Finally, positive attitudes and negative attitudes become separated and more consistent with the reality that motivates them. The intensity of feelings accompanying these stages also seems to change. First the feelings of anger are severe in nature. Then they become less intense in their expression, and finally they appear to be more moderate.

Anxiety may be looked at in the same way. In the beginning of child therapy, anxiety may be diffuse and the child may be generally withdrawn and frightened, tense and garrulous, or overanxious about being clean, neat, or orderly. This attitude is often so pervasive that the child is immobilized and unable to start anything, or complete anything, or even to think clearly and attack problems logically. He does not seem to know how to go about doing what he really wants to do. Fears also may take other forms, such as regular night terrors or bizarre fears of animals and things. In the first stage of the therapeutic process, fears seem to obsess the child. At the next level, they take on more specific aspects. Fears of the father or the mother or some other particular person are expressed again and again. Fear then becomes mixed with positive attitudes, becomes milder in its expression. Finally positive and negative attitudes toward particular people become separated and more in line with the actual situation. Here again, negative feeling tones change from severe to moderate.

The child's emotional problems and symptoms are reflections of his attitudes, and as the attitudes change the problems and symptoms disappear. It must be remembered that these levels of the process and the changes in feeling tones are not distinct entities or even always definitely observable. They occur in the child's play and in his emotional behavior, not step by step, but in individually varying sequences. The levels overlap at many points, as do the children's attitudes themselves. On the other hand, they are definite sequences of the process which can be observed and understood.

The therapeutic process does not automatically occur in a play situation. It becomes possible in a therapeutic relationship where the therapist responds in constant sensitivity to the child's feelings, accepts the child's attitudes, and conveys a consistent and sincere belief in the child and respect for him.

CHAPTER II

Preventive Play Therapy–A Mental Hygiene Program

The Merrill-Palmer School offers a program in play therapy for all children enrolled in the nursery school. Every child is given an opportunity to express freely feelings about himself and others in his life. Those children with disturbing emotions have a chance to work them out. The program is a cooperative effort between the nursery school and the guidance service. Parents, too, play an important role in this program.

THE PARENTS

An attempt is made, at various times during the school year, to introduce individual parents and occasionally groups of parents to the philosophy, approaches, and techniques of play therapy and to familiarize them with some of its goals. The parents have an opportunity to ask questions and make critical evaluations.

Parents may visit the playroom, examine the play material and the concealed observation room. They are shown the hidden microphones.. The recording machine is pointed out to them, and the methods of recording and transcribing play sessions are described. Recordings of child therapy sessions have been played and parents encouraged to discuss the behavioral patterns of particular children in play situations. They have commented on how they felt

10

about these children. Some have introduced their own family experiences and discussed them with other parents.

Parents are interested in play therapy. They ask many questions about it. They want to know how normal children as well as disturbed children may benefit. They ask about the materials and their arrangement in the room. They want to know how children use the toys in their play. They are curious about the therapist, what he does and how he reacts. They are especially interested in when and how limits are set and how they are maintained. They sometimes express a desire to discuss their children's play experiences with the therapist.

Often parents are encouraged to explore further the feelings around their questions. At other times their questions are answered simply as requests for information. Parents are urged to feel free to request appointments to discuss their children at any time.

When parents are given an opportunity to understand and participate in the experiences of their children in play therapy, they become very enthusiastic. They show strong motivation for recognition and clarification of their children's emotions. Most parents seem to accept the fact that emotional frustrations and disturbances in children are frequently motivated by an impairment in family relationships which often is rooted in early family experiences. They understand that a troubled child may have a history of experiences where he was made to feel incapable, insecure, and inadequate, and that these feelings of worthlessness often pervade everything the child does and prevent him from functioning effectively. Many parents accept the idea that feelings of inferiority may arouse anger and guilt and fear, and that the more severe the child's sense of personal unworthiness and rejection, the more likely is he to have deep underlying feelings of anxiety and hostility. These strong negative attitudes toward the self and others seem to prevent the child from fully utilizing his inner resources in his relationships with other people and with ideas. They seem to create psychological problems and often bizarre and terrifying symptoms.

Parents are encouraged to believe that no matter how many mistakes they have made and how insensitive and nonresponsive they have been, it is still possible to help the child release his intense negative feelings and through a therapeutic relationship to help him grow emotionally and use his abilities toward happier, more rewarding experiences with other children and adults.

THE SCHEDULE

All children have frustrating and tension-producing experiences which they cannot easily express in the home or at school. .All children have inner motivations which they cannot easily reveal under ordinary conditions. The policy, therefore, is to schedule every nursery school child for at least three individual play therapy sessions and one group therapy session a week apart. Scheduling is a joint enterprise between the nursery school and the guidance service. At the time of initial scheduling, the nursery school staff presents a brief report of the personal and social adjustments of each child who was in nursery school the previous year. These reports are often used as a basis for scheduling.

The oldest nursery school child is seen first and then the next oldest, down to the youngest child. The schedule is kept flexible. It may be changed at any time. The nursery school department may request that a child be seen earlier or later than previously arranged. A parent may call and make a similar request. Sometimes the children themselves make requests which necessitate changes in the schedule. Any child who wishes to return for play therapy after the usual number of sessions may express this desire either to the therapist or to his nursery school teacher. This opportunity for further contacts is explained to each child sometime during his play therapy experiences.

Conferences are frequently held between the nursery school and guidance service staffs. Together they make recommendations for further therapeutic contacts in the cases of disturbed children.

FIRST CONTACTS WITH THE CHILD

Before the child comes to the playroom, he is introduced to the therapist by his teacher. The therapist then observes the child in the nursery school and attempts to establish rapport with him. On the day the child is scheduled for a play session, the therapist approaches him with such an expression as, "Hello, Bobby. It's your turn to come over and play in the playroom today."

Bobby may not wish to come on that day, or he may not be able to decide. If he is uncertain, the therapist may say, "You want to come to the playroom and yet you want to stay here, too," waiting for Bobby to make the decision. It is especially important at this time that the child himself decides whether or not he wishes to come to the playroom. Whatever decision the child makes is accepted by the therapist. If the child refuses, the therapist may say, "I see. You don't want to come to the playroom today. I shall ask you again another time."

This belief in the child's ability to make decisions for himself is maintained in every contact with the child. When this attitude is firmly held, the children, both normal and disturbed, will more often than not decide to come for play therapy when they feel a need for it.

The Playroom and Materials

The playroom is a brightly colored, cheerful room. The materials are arranged in an unstructured fashion. There is no attempt to indicate the identity of the toys or the contexts in which to use them. Trucks, cars, guns, knives, airplanes, sea divers, hot-water bottles, telephones, boats, and tractors are placed on shelves. Hand puppets, shovels, bowls, spoons, dolls, and a jump rope may also be found in the room. Crayons, clay, finger paint, paper, scissors, steel vises, and plastic aprons are important items. A large dollhouse, doll furniture, and a number of doll figures are located in a corner of the room. In addition to these materials, there are also nursing bottles, lead soldiers, sand, water, easel paints, masks, blocks, balloons, and a comeback toy (a large figurelike balloon weighted at the bottom).

Actually, the number of toys in the room is not too important. The main factor is that they be arranged in an unstructured fashion, so that the child is not pressured or forced into using them in any particular way. The child should feel free to project his own feelings and attitudes onto the items in the room and to use them in whatever manner he chooses.

Stability in Materials and Relationship

The materials and the relationship in play therapy remain stable. The playthings are always arranged in the same way each time the child enters the room. The attitudes of the therapist remain consistent, too. The materials and the relationship, then, are the steady forces which act upon the child. Outside the playroom, the child lives in a changing world where others are responsible for the changes. In the playroom, he is the guide. He makes the changes.

As therapy progresses, the materials and the therapist's attitudes may appear different to the child as a result of his changing perceptions, understandings, and meanings. In reality these are constant patterns and serve as sources of strength for the child.

Structuring the Relationship

During the early phases of play therapy, structuring is a very important process. It involves introducing the child to the playroom and creating a warm, permissive relationship. It is partly through structuring that the therapist conveys attitudes of faith, acceptance, and respect to the child. Structuring also assists the child in gaining impressions of the quality of the therapeutic relationship.

The therapist may use any of the following expressions: "You may use these in any way that you want," "It can be anything you want it to be," "I can't decide that for you; the important thing is that you decide for yourself what you want to do," "You want me to tell you what that is. Well, whatever you want to make it," "You want me to do that for you, Janey, but here you do things for yourself." Through the structured relationship, the child is able to achieve a clear understanding of his freedom and to state himself in his own terms.

Reflection of Feelings

The primary purpose in reflecting feelings is to indicate empathy to the child, to further encourage him to express and explore his feelings. This empathetic sharing of an experience shows the child that his feelings are understood and accepted. Reflections themselves, without these values in mind, have very little effect on the child's growth. True reflections of feelings result only from a close following of the child's attitudes and an understanding of their implications.

The therapist maintains a listening attitude. Listening requires careful attention and consideration not merely to content but, more significantly, to the feelings. Listening is an active process. Feelings can be heard. The therapist must be a sensitive, discerning listener. He must not get lost in his own attitudes or thoughts. Reflection reinforces the attitudes of faith, acceptance, and respect which are the main goals of the therapeutic relationship.

Setting of Limits

One of the most important aspects of play therapy is the setting of limits. Limits bind the relationship and tie it to reality. Without limits there would be no therapy. The limits define the boundaries of the relationship. There are certain things the child must not do. The limits serve to remind him of his responsibilities to the therapist, the playroom, and himself. They offer security and at the same time permit the child to move freely and safely in his play. They make the playroom experiences a living reality.

A time limit is always set in child therapy. Usually it is a forty-five minute period. The therapist indicates the time limit briefly. He lets the child know when he has only a few minutes left to play and at the end of the period says, "I see that our time is up for today. We'll have to stop now."

There are limits in the use of materials. They must be used only in the playroom. They may not be taken home. "I know you want to take that home but you have to use it here." Certain expensive or irreplaceable items may not be destroyed.

Realistically enough, the child is not permitted to abuse physically the therapist or his clothing. "You really want to smear me with the paint, but that is one of the things I cannot let you do here."

Once the child decides to leave before a session has ended, he may not come back into the playroom on that day. "You can go now if you want; it's up to you. If you go, though, I cannot let you come back today."

These conditions may be thought of as reality and psychological security limits which act as a safeguard for the child. Without these limits the child would be forced to move in threatening and unfamiliar emotional areas which might stimulate anxiety and arouse guilt. These externally induced feelings might create a barrier in the relationship. In addition to the reality and security limits, there are also a few health and safety limits. The therapist might say, "It would be fun to smash that bottle against the wall, but I can't let you do that," or "Billy and Jack, you may play with the sand in other ways, but you may not throw it in each other's faces."

As with all limits, there are other health and safety limits that may have to be set in the course of therapy. The therapist himself must then make the distinction between permissiveness and practical reality. In most instances, children accept these limits. Occasionally a child insists on breaking a limit. The therapist must then decide what to do to enforce the limit. He may place a toy or area of the room out of bounds, or stand by the child and repeat the limit, or hold the child a few minutes. As a last measure, he may have to carry the child out of the playroom, ending the therapy session. Whatever the therapist does, he should continue to help the child feel accepted even though he cannot be permitted to do certain things.

It is through these processes of structuring, reflection, and setting of limits that therapy becomes more than just a theoretical postulate. It becomes a warm, practical, living experience. It enables a group of growing children to live their emotional lives more freely and fully. It helps them to be alive and unafraid, so that they give more of their true selves to themselves and to society.

CHAPTER III

Play Therapy with Normal Children

Play therapy presents a unique experience for normal children. It offers a relationship in a situation where the boundaries are greatly expanded. In the playroom children can feel their feelings completely. They can express hatred, fear, and anger, be resentful and disgusted or hilarious, joyous, and silly. They can be fully themselves. They can be babies at one moment who speak a garbled language and act immaturely and later their own age without fear of being examined and criticized. In fantasy they can be grown men and women who tell people what to do and how to do it. They may assume many different family roles if they wish. They can be, in their imaginative play, anything they want to be.

In the playroom these children need not submit to the everyday pressures of their school and family environments. They are free to explore whatever feelings, attitudes, and minor problems and frustrations they wish. The therapeutic relationship does not set up standards or social values for them. It honors every impulse, need, and projection as it is expressed.

How Normal Children Approach and Use Play Therapy

Not all normal children use the therapy experience in the same way. Each child has his own symbols for expressing himself and his own way of perceiving and reacting to the relationship. There are, however, certain general characteristics which are frequently observed in the play behavior of normal children in a therapeutic relationship.

Normal children are conversational and prone at various times during their play contacts to discuss their world directly as it exists for them. They are free and spontaneous in their play. They examine the whole play setting and use a large variety of play materials in a well-organized fashion and often in unique, original ways.

When they are bothered or annoyed, they usually bring out the problem in their play in a rather concrete way. Normal children do not hesitate to express aggressive and regressive impulses. Their aggression is clearly expressed, and responsibility is taken for it. They are not usually timid, subtle, or fearful, nor are they violent, cunning, or sadistic in their expressions. They at times show immaturity and use baby talk and gibberish but ordinarily leave this behavior and move on to what, for them, is a more rewarding type of behavior for their development.

Normal children almost immediately look upon the therapist as a special kind of person. They use various strategies to discover their responsibilities and limitations in the therapeutic relationship. They seem happy in their play, often singing and humming. They are not so serious and intense in their feelings as disturbed children, about themselves, the therapist, or their play.

Other differences may be noted. Normal children are more decisive and spontaneous than disturbed children. Whereas disturbed children frequently express anger and other strong emotions in a diffused way, these same emotions are localized and focused more clearly by the normal child. Disturbed children tend to be more suspicious and resentful of the therapist, especially in the early interviews, while normal children quickly establish a freely trusting relationship. Normal children often discuss their play therapy experiences with teachers and parents, including regressive and aggressive aspects of behavior. Disturbed children, on the other hand, very rarely discuss their play experiences outside the playroom.

The most important aspect of the play therapy experience for the normal child is the concentrated relationship with the therapist, created in a short span of time. In this relationship the child is able to express whatever minor frustrations or resentments he may feel and to bring out whatever aggressive or regressive behavior he may wish. In this respect, play therapy is a type of preventive program of mental hygiene for normal children. They use it as a way of growing in their own self-acceptance and respect and also as a way of looking at attitudes that might not be easily explored in school or at home.

Three examples are presented to illustrate the characteristics and uses of play therapy with normal children. These children displayed some attitudes in play therapy that their teachers had not observed or recognized as part of their personalities. Discussions will follow the verbatim recordings presented in this and other chapters of the book. It should be remembered that the discussions, though presented with definiteness, are offered only as tentative explanations and impressions. The reader is encouraged to substitute insights and modifications of his own upon examination of the case material.

JOHNNY

Johnny, a highly active four-year-old, eagerly entered the playroom. For the first ten minutes he talked about family experiences and some of his activities of the past few weeks. He attempted to discover what kind of relationship this was going to be. He made his decision about the relationship and then, seemingly satisfied, moved on to play. He went directly to the dollhouse and put furniture into the various rooms of the house. He whistled and sang throughout the session. During his imaginative play he told amusing stories about unusual incidents.

Johnny ordinarily expresses himself in letter-perfect English. His vocabulary is extensive for a four-year-old, yet here in the playroom he regresses and uses baby talk and peculiar-sounding syllables. His regressive impulses are recognized by the therapist and accepted as they are expressed. Johnny feels free to be what he wants to be; to be little and to be big.

The excerpt which follows describes initially some regressive patterns and, later, some very unusual imaginative play.

FIRST PLAY SESSION WITH JOHNNY

CHILD: (*Walks to the nursing bottles. Picks up a bottle and puts it into his mouth. Sucks on nipple for a few seconds, then replaces bottle.*) I want to take another little drink of that.

THERAPIST: You want to have another little drink, hm?

C: Yeah. (*Picks up the bottle and drinks again.*) I'm gonna take one more sip.

T: You've decided to take one more sip.

C: I'm gonna take a big sip this time—a great big one. (*Takes a long drink from the bottle. Replaces bottle on the bench and walks to the dollhouse. Picks up a boy doll figure and a small rubber cat. Shouts in a baby voice.*) Whoo, whoo, whoo. Meow, meow, meow, meow. (*Holds figures over the roof of dollhouse.*) Kitty gonna jump. Baby gonna jump. Kitty jump down. Baby jump down. See-shee, see-shee, see-shee, see-shee. (*A few minutes later picks up a woman doll.*) She's a Girl Scout, and here she is. She runs with a whip. She runs with a whip.

T: Running, running, running.

C: Running. Yes, and she's ice skating, ice skating. She ice skates wherever she goes. Skating all around. (*Picks up a rubber knife.*) And there's her carving knife. She carves, she carves with her carving knife. And she carves and carves and carves.

T: She carves with her carving knife, hm?

C: Yeah. She wears metal ice skates only on the ice. She skates without any clothes on, because it's warm ice. (*Removes clothing from doll.*)

T: She just doesn't need to wear any.

C: No, no. It's spring ice. It's in the spring, so she goes around with no things on. She skates everywhere with nothing on. (*Handles doll and twists and turns it into many different positions.*) See? See? She's still ice skating. She's gonna ice

skate the whole morning. She skates everywhere she goes.
There she goes on the ice. Twisting and turning.

T: Twisting and turning.

C: And sliding.

T: And sliding, too. She can do all sorts of things.

C: Yeah. Lookit.

T: Mm-hm.

C: See how she goes. She goes like this and like that. And you
know? She always carries a knife, and she holds her knife.
And when she's ice skating she can stick it through the ice
and slice the fish. She just jumps and—whee! There's a hole,
and she sticks her knife into it and catches the fish.

T: She really enjoys ice skating and fishing.

C: She fishes through the ice. See? She kneels down, and she
ice skates, and when she wants to catch the fish, she does.
And then when she catches the fish, she's happy. Then,
see? She dances.

T: Mm-hm. She dances and dances. She's so happy.

Discussion: First Play Session

We see in this session that Johnny's basic negative attitude is
regression. He sucks from the nursing bottle, replaces it, then takes
another drink. There is no impelling urgency to drink, nor is there
hesitancy and uncertainty. His feelings of need are not intense.
Johnny's second negative expression is also an attitude of regression. His speech becomes immature, and his voice is on a higher
pitch. Johnny then switches to a more mature type of behavior,
expressing himself in a unique way, humming and singing and ob-
viously very happy. His imaginative play is accepted just as it is
expressed, and the values lying within it are respected. Here in
the playroom, Johnny's ice skater can skate without clothes on
warm ice.

In a later session Johnny revealed that he himself was the skater
whom he so happily described. Johnny threw off his clothing,
spilled water on the floor, and skated around the room. Every once
in a while, with knife in hand, he lunged toward the floor, catching fish and screaming gleefully.

MICHAEL

Michael, four years old, is described by his nursery school teacher as "a youngster who is most frequently seen with other children. He is an enthusiastic leader of his age group. He has had a steady interest in more structured, organized groups and activities. He usually operates independently of adults in these situations. He becomes irritated with adults who interfere with his games or activities. He shows little tendency for solitary play except when he becomes absorbed in books or records. Most of his play is of a very creative sort, advanced for his age. His relations with adults are quite good, and he shares many of his special interests with them. He seems free in expressing verbal aggression toward adults and is not particularly worried about returning to their good graces."

Two individual sessions and one group session were conducted with Michael. During the first he was quite conversational in describing recent family experiences. He expressed some aggression by kicking and hitting the comeback toy. He explored his father's attitude of rigidly sticking to certain limits and his own feelings about it. He also showed warm, positive identification with his father. During the second session Michael regressed by using the nursing bottle and sucking on it. He later took the responsibility for this behavior by informing the therapist that he could tell anyone that he (Michael) had been drinking from the bottle. He also showed that he was bothered somewhat by the death of a neighbor.

After the second session Michael said he did not want to come back any more, but a month later asked if he might come with a group. In the group session Michael spilled water around the room and led two other children in almost every activity. They looked to him for help continually during the session. They did whatever he asked them to do. Sometimes he suggested that the other children break things in the room, and later he joined in this activity, breaking two balloons himself. He spent the last ten minutes of the group session painting and drawing, and the other children joined him in this activity.

Transcripts from tape recordings of the two individual sessions follow.

First Play Sessions with Michael

T: You can use these in any way you like, Michael.

C: O.K. (*Points to a small gun on the table.*) My brother used to have a gun just like this one.

T: He had a gun like that, hm?

C: Yes. Except that it wasn't filled up with clay like that one.

T: Mm-hm.

C: (*For the next seven minutes C plays quietly, shooting the gun and pushing cars and trucks around the table. Toward the end of this time he walks to the doll furniture.*) I used to have little things like these.

T: You did, hm?

C: (*Plays silently with the doll furniture, arranging the furniture in the rooms of the dollhouse. Ten minutes later he takes all the furniture out of the house and looks at the therapist.*) I have to go-go.

T: You have to go, hm? All right.

C: (*Comes back from bathroom and pats comeback toy on head. Holds shirt in hand and then puts it on.*) I don't know why Mommy wants me to wear a sweater in the house. Like here, or some place like that where it's warm. She always says, "Put it on, put it on." I don't know why she wants me to, but she just does.

T: It's hard to understand.

C: (*Pause.*) I used to have a little telephone like this.

T: You had one like that.

C: Mm-hm. 'Cept it wasn't this heavy. It was light. (*Picks up a rubber airplane.*) If this were made out of wood or a little lighter, it would really fly.

T: Go right up in the air, hm?

C: If it was just made a little fatter like my father's, and a big storm came, it would really fly. It would fly right up in the air like a gas balloon, and it would stay up. It would stay up, too.

T: You mean it would never come down?

C: Maybe it would come down, but I *know* it would fly. And if a big storm came—a big, big, *big* one—then you could just see it floating up there, and it would stay up a long time.

T: Mm-hm.

C: (*Points to the comeback toy.*) Is this a big balloon?

T: You make it whatever you want to.

C: What's in it that makes it so heavy? Is there just air in it?

T: It's just filled up.

C: With air. (*Hits at comeback toy.*) I really knocked it.

T: You really did knock it.

C: (*Pushes comeback toy down on the floor and sits on it.*) It's a chair now, and I'm sitting on it. Look. I'm riding on a balloon. (*Slides off comeback, grabs it and hugs it. Then kicks it around the room. Finally leaves it and picks up a small green balloon.*) You know, you can get lots more balloons, and I know where. At the dime store.

T: You could buy all you want there.

C: Yeah. 'Cause they keep bringing them and bringing more. These people do. They go pop, and you can get more.

T: Sometimes people break them, but you can always get more.

C: Yes. You know, once mine broke, and my daddy could have gotten me some more, but he wouldn't. He didn't want to.

T: Yours broke once, and your daddy didn't want to get you any more.

C: He could have. He could have if he had wanted to, but he just didn't want to.

T: Just wouldn't get you any more, though you would have liked him to.

C: Yes. (*Pause.*) (*Lifts roof of dollhouse.*) How did you make it so it would go up like that?

T: You wonder about that, hm?

C: Why did you make it go that way? So people could get a little air?

T: It might be used for that, mightn't it?

C: Yes. The firemen could use it. They could get in.

T: Mm-hm.

C: (*Leaves dollhouse and picks up a balloon.*) If I was outside, I could sling this around, and it would stay up, and it would float a long time.

T: Float in the air and stay right up.

C: (*Points to the masks.*) What are those for?

T: You can do whatever you want with them.

C: They're rubber, huh? I'm gonna put them on once and scare you.

T: You feel like scaring me.

C: Yes. I'm gonna put them all on and scare you. (*Puts each of the masks on.*)

T: Now you've scared me with all of them.

C: Yes. I've scared you with the monkey and the clown and the pig. Do you have any more here?

T: No, that's all we have.

C: Well, you know you could get some more.

T: Could we buy more?

C: *I* think you could.

T: You believe we could, hm?

C: Yes. (*Pause.*)

T: You have only a short while longer to play, Mike, and then you'll have to stop for today.

C: Why?

T: Because your time is almost up over here.

C: O.K. You know? The monkey looks the funniest of them all. Do you want to put it on?

T: Do you suppose I do?

C: Yes. (*Puts the monkey mask on the therapist and laughs. Pulls the mask off therapist and replaces it on bench. Goes to lead soldiers.*) What are they doing?

T: Just whatever you decide.

C: Well, I think they're flying. They're flying right up. (*Leaves soldiers and picks up a nursing bottle. Examines it and then puts it back on bench. Returns to lead figures and points to the policeman figure.*) What's he doing?

T: You tell me.

C: Oh, he's just policing. How are they made?

T: What would you say about that?

C: With lead. (*Walks to the comeback toy.*) I'm gonna give him a good big kick and try to knock him down. See? There he goes.

T: You kicked him down that time.

C: Mm-hm. Twice.

T: Well, I see your time is up for now, so I'll take you back to the nursery school, Mike.

C: O.K. (*Leaves room with therapist.*)

Discussion: First Play Session

In this session we see that Michael first expresses a negative attitude of a mild nature. Michael resents his mother's rule that he wear a sweater in the house. Next he expresses a minor negative attitude toward his father, who refused to buy Michael a new balloon after he had broken one. Later he tries to get the therapist to support him in his feeling that when balloons are broken they can be easily replaced. These mild expressions of resentment may seem somewhat unimportant. Yet to Michael it was very important to express these feelings and to be heard and accepted. There is also an indication of a desire to be more aggressive without being punished.

SECOND PLAY SESSION WITH MICHAEL

C: (*Walks into the room and points to pail of water.*) What's this for?

T: You can use it for anything you want.

C: (*During the next fifteen minutes Michael plays quietly with the airplanes and the soldiers. Then goes to the dollhouse, puts all the furniture in, and places all the doll figures on beds. Opens roof of the dollhouse, then walks to a large balloon and picks it up.*) This one is just about ready to go up. If I let it go like this, if there was only a little water in it, then it would really go up. Like a blimp. And if I had air to blow it, then it could be a jet. It could be a jet.

T: It could be a jet, couldn't it?

C: (*Pause.*) Did you go to camp last Sunday?

T: No, I didn't.

C: Well, you should have seen my dad's plane fly. It went clear up in the sky. It might have crashed if a real plane had gone by.

T: You were afraid that it might have crashed, huh?

C: Well, it might have. I don't know if it would have, but it

didn't. (*Continues to toss balloon in the air.*) There now.
It's ready. I'll see if it will fly.

T: You're trying to fly it.

C: Yes. But it's too heavy. It won't stay. (*Pause.*) This is a real
nice place here.

T: You like it over here, hm?

C: Mm-hm. That balloon is going to pop.

T: It will pop?

C: No. I'm just teasing you. But maybe it would happen. Who
knows?

T: It might.

C: (*Empties water from small nursing bottle into pail by squeezing nipple.*) I can fill it up with more water.

T: You could do that if you wanted to.

C: (*Takes large nursing bottle and ejects water into pail by squeezing nipple.*) This is music. It sounds like music. Yup. Just
like music. (*Puts bottle in mouth and drinks from it.
Squeezes more water into pail, then drinks from bottle
again. Points to the nursing bottle.*) Look. Look how far
down it's gone. Maybe I'll put a little more in and fill it up.

T: Maybe you will and maybe you won't.

C: Who knows? Do you want to drink from it?

T: No.

C: Then I'll give him (*comeback toy*) a drink. If he had a big
hole, I'd really put water in him, and he'd get much heavier.
And maybe if I got him wet, he would go pop.

T: Just go pop, that's what.

C: You know? You could give this stuff to a cow.

T: You could do that.

C: (*Sits down on the floor and moves one hand up and down in
pail of water while using the other hand to hold the bottle
in his mouth. Points to the bottle.*) You know, to get this
room filled with this, it takes millions and trillions of days.

T: A long time, hm?

C: A very long time.

T: A long, long time.

C: It would take near to the end of counting, and I would get so
tired.

T: You'd be worn out.

C: It would take so long that I couldn't stay alive that long.

T: You couldn't live that long, hm?

C: No. On the fifteenth day I'd be a father, and on the fiftieth day I'd be an old man.

T: Just an old man, that's what.

C: Like my neighbor. You know, he died last week. He died. The last day on the calendar he died. Just last week he died.

T: Just like that he died.

C: (*Long silence.*)

T: You have only a short while longer to play, Michael.

C: I bet people will ask you who drank from here and poured all that into the pail.

T: Someone might ask those questions.

C: And then what would you say?

T: What would you want me to tell them?

C: Say that Michael T. did it.

T: All right. I'll say that to them.

C: Probably they've never seen me. And anyway, they wouldn't understand.

T: They wouldn't understand, hm?

C: (*Pause.*) You've got so many toys in here. Where did you get all of them?

T: The school buys them for the playroom.

C: I'd like to take some, but then there wouldn't be enough to play with. And besides, you wouldn't let me take them.

T: You don't think I'd let you take them?

C: We wouldn't have enough to play with if I did.

T: That's true.

C: It would be just like it was all food and I ate it. Then there wouldn't be anything for anyone else.

T: It would be just like that.

C: Look at your wrist watch and see if it's time to go.

T: We have a few more minutes left.

C: Well, I'm ready to go now. I'm finished.

T: O.K.

Discussion: Second Play Session

Michael expresses positive feelings and identification with his father. He proudly describes his dad's model planes. He plays immaturely, drinking from the nursing bottle and squeezing the nipple.

Michael's sensitivity to people is brought out in a number of instances, most dramatically perhaps in his comment that taking the toys away from the playroom would be like eating food: when it was all gone, there wouldn't be anything for anyone else.

The nursery school staff expressed surprise that Michael had used the nursing bottle during his play sessions and indicated that they had not seen regressive behavior of this kind in the nursery school. His teacher indicated that there had been no noticeable change in Michael's behavior after his play sessions. Michael told both his teacher and his mother, pretty much in detail, what had happened in the playroom. He also mentioned that he had enjoyed the experience.

Joey

Joey, three and one-half years old, was described by his nursery school teacher as a happy, carefree child who played well with other children and who also engaged in individual activities with initiative and confidence. His relationships with adults were quite good, and only rarely did he lose control or have difficulty accepting limits in school. According to intelligence test findings he rated superior, and he was well advanced for his age in vocabulary achievement. Joey has an eight-year-old brother and a two-year-old sister.

Joey came into the playroom three times, the sessions a week apart. He seemed from the beginning to be an uninhibited child who engaged in activities with confidence. The therapist's goal from the first moment was to establish in these three sessions a secure relationship with Joey in which the main communications were faith, acceptance, and respect.

At the beginning of his first session Joey revealed indecisiveness by asking what he should do. After twenty minutes he said, "I didn't know what I was going to do when I came in, did I?" indicating then that he was able to make decisions. Joey also expressed some aggression against the comeback toy, attacking it and rolling on the floor with it. At the same time he showed affection for the huge balloon figure by hugging it and holding it close to him. Toward the end of the first session Joey struggled with the problem of whether he should get paint on his hands. After a long time of feeling it through and trying other approaches, he himself decided that he would paint with his hands—"I'll put all my fingers in there to get some out."

FIRST PLAY SESSION WITH JOEY

T: You can use these in any way that you want, Joey.

C: Guns. And look! That's clay.

T: Mm-hm.

C: (*Picks up a cat balloon.*) Hey! See?

T: Mm-hm.

C: What's this? Is this a kitty cat?

T: Do you suppose that's what it is?

C: It looks like a kitty cat. (*Squeezes balloon and drops it to floor. Picks up three other balloons.*) What are these for?

T: You can use them in any way that you want.

C: (*Looks at balloons for a few seconds, then drops them on the floor. Picks one up again.*) How did this one get so dirty?

T: How would you explain it, Joey?

C: (*Sighs heavily and shrugs shoulders. Picks up a knife and sucks on the handle for a few seconds, then bites on the knife blade. Moves to dollhouse and picks up a male doll figure.*) What's this?

T: Whatever you want it to be.

C: (*Undresses a number of boy and girl doll figures.*) This is a girl and these are her shoes. And this is something else. It's a boy. (*Takes out men and women figures and starts to undress them.*) That. That. Take off his coat. Take off his jacket. Take his hand up like that and pull it like that. And here is the baby.

T: That's the baby, hm?

C: The baby, the baby. You take it off like this and like this. And here's another baby. And this is the mommy, and this is the little boy. And this one's the girl. She's the mommy. (*Pause.*) Let's go to toidy.

T: You have to go?

C: Uh-huh.

T: All right.

C: (*Goes to the bathroom with therapist. Returns and picks up a balloon.*) You know, there should be a string here at the tail end. There should be a string to tie around all of these.

T: We should have strings for that, hm?

C: Yes. Look. You can see right through this one. But this one— it's sure dusty. You can't look through this one. See?

T: Kind of dusty, isn't it?

C: (*Walks to table and picks up ball of clay. Inserts some clay in vise.*) Do you have any sticks here? Look. I'm turning this around and around in here. See? And I'm turning it over here and down here and back to here.

T: Mm-hm. You're making it go all over.

C: (*Pulls a small piece off ball of clay and grunts. Then starts pushing on the clay.*)

T: You're pushing it as hard as you can.

C: Yes. (*Grunts again.*) There. I'm gonna take a piece off. I'm gonna break a piece off. Little pieces off. See? I broke a piece. It's large enough.

T: It is, hm?

C: Yes. It's large enough. I just breaked it off.

T: You just pull it right off.

C: I need some new pieces. And then you can roll it right up like this.

T: You just roll it and roll it and roll it.

C: It's hard. (*Holds a piece of clay. Picks up a large gun and shoots at clay.*)

T: Bang.

C: (*Puts gun down and walks over to comeback toy and hits it.*)

T: Socko.

C: Woooo. (*Pushes comeback toy down and sits on it. Bounces up and down on comeback's head and begins to breathe more heavily. Gets off comeback toy and watches it rise.*) It got up. Up.

T: It shot right back up.

C: (*Looks at comeback toy for a few seconds. Then sits on it and starts to hit it. Lies on the comeback and rolls around on the floor.*) You know, I didn't know what I was going to do when I came in, did I?

T: You didn't know then, but now you know what you want to do.

C: I didn't know what I was going to play—play down here.

T: You didn't, hm?

C: (*Picks up gun and shoots comeback toy in the head.*) I shot the clown.

T: You shot the clown.

C: (*Shoots comeback again.*)

T: Bang.

C: I shot it right in his mouth. He can't talk now.

T: Right in the mouth so he'll never say anything.

C: No.

T: He'll just keep quiet.

C: Yeah. (*Goes back to the clay. Pulls a piece off and grunts.*) I took a piece.

T: Mm-hm.

C: (*Starts rolling long pieces of clay.*) You take this, and you do this.

T: Mm-hm.

C: That's the way you do it. That way and that. See?

T: Mm-hm.

C: (*Picks up gun again and shoots at clay.*)

T: Bang.

C: (*Goes to finger paints and opens jar of yellow paint. Starts to pour some of it on the paper.*) There's not little paintbrushes here, is there?

T: No, we don't have any brushes in here, Joey.

C: (*Looks at paint on paper.*) How am I going to do that?

T: That's hard to figure out, isn't it?

C: (*Picks up scissors and moves them up and down in the yellow paint.*) Take it like this.

T: Mm-hm.

C: And then a little bit like this. (*Opens jar of blue paint and uses scissors to put some of the paint on the paper.*) Look.

T: Mm-hm.

C: It's deep. Now I'll stir it up a little. See? I didn't get paint on me, so I can use the scissors.

T: You don't want to get any paint on you, hm?

C: Uh-huh. I don't want to get it on my sweater, so I'll just have to use this. (*Rubs scissors back and forth on paint-smeared paper.*) There. Lookit.

T: You've got it all on now, hm?

C: You do this way. I have to do it.

T: Mm-hm. That's the way you have to do it.

C: I can't do it with my two hands.

T: You can't?

C: Yes. I can. (*Smears paint over paper with hands and starts to make figures.*) I can go to the bathroom, can't I?

T: If you want to. It's up to you.

C: Mm-hm. When I'm through. More paint with the scissors. More paint now. You know, the paint's pretty near gone. (*Uses the scissors to take more paint out of jars and smears it on the paper.*) Look. There's only two scissorsful left.

T: Only that much, hm?

C: You know what I should do? I should go and get some water and make some more paint.

T: That's what you want to do. Make more paint.

C: Mm-hm.

T: You have only a short while longer to play, Joey, and then we have to go back.

C: (*Pounds the clay on paper and cuts clay with scissors.*) You do it like this and then like that.

T: You pound it, hm?

C: And you cut it like this and then this. Like this.

T: Mm-hm.

C: And then in the center like that. You make a little hole there like that. You know what I should do? I should take my fingers and take it out like this.

T: You feel like doing it that way now.

C: That way. (*Sticks fingers into jar of blue paint and starts painting pieces of clay.*) This way. And this way and this and this. Just like this. I can get it out with my hand and my fingers. You take it out just like this.

T: You can take it out that way.

C: I'll get it out. My big hand's in the way. I'll put all my fingers in there to get some out. (*Finishes painting clay and then smears paint over the paper.*) Gotta paint 'em. Where should we put this to hang?

T: You mean you want to hang it up to dry?

C: I know where we can put it. We can put it right over here. Hang it up so it can be dry and pretty.

T: It can be dry and pretty then, hm?

C: You know, you should get pink paint at the store.

T: Pink paint?

C: Yes. So I can make a pink painting.

T: You'd like to do a pink painting, hm?

C: Yes.

T: Well, Joey, your time is up now.

C: Some day when I come again, I'm going to look and look until I find the pink paint.

Discussion: First Play Session

Joey's regression is most prominent in this session. It is expressed largely in his sucking, biting, and grunting behavior. He also shows some aggression, shooting frequently at the clay and later at the comeback. His expression of hostility toward the clown indicates strong accompanying feelings. He is careful to shoot the clown in the mouth so that "he can't talk now," thereby removing the possibility that the clown will report his behavior. He then feels free to continue his immature behavior. One might assume that the clown represents some person in his life who may be critical in some ways of Joey as a person. Joey perhaps rejects his own immaturity by shooting at the clay which he has used to symbolize his immature impulses.

In the following session Joey's patterns of behavior were primarily regressive. He spoke baby talk and gibberish, sucked and chewed on the nipple, and drank from the nursing bottle. The therapist accepted this behavior and encouraged him to continue to explore it. His play was much freer than in the first session, and he was quite unconcerned about the clay which he had gotten all over his hands. Joey expressed hostility toward the therapist in his desire to smear him with clay but accepted the limit that was placed on him. Aggression was expressed also in the burying of the dog in clay. After gaining satisfaction from burying the dog and pounding the clay and cutting into the buried dog with the scissors, he pulled the dog from the clay and moved the dog around the room, happily making loud barking sounds.

SECOND PLAY SESSION WITH JOEY

C: (*Enters and goes immediately to the vise. Touches it and walks away. Pulls out a number of items from his pocket.*) I brought these over.

T: Oh, I see. You brought over a few things of your own this time.

C: Mm-hm. I brought them over 'cause I wanted to.

T: You not only wanted to bring them, but you did.

C: Mm-hm. I'm not gonna play with none of these things. I'm just gonna put them in my pocket with the rest. O.K.?

T: You're going to put them all in there.

C: (*Picks up a large gun and shoots it.*)

T: Bang.

C: (*Walks to dollhouse and shoots through one of the windows.*)

T: Bang.

C: Oh, lookit. Here's a doggy. A doggy. (*Shoots the gun at the dog figure.*)

T: Bang. You shot the doggy.

C: I did that, but I didn't do it really, did I?

T: Just pretending, hm?

C: Mm-hm. I've got a gun at home. Not like that, though. Another kind. I have a gun, and it twists, and then it comes down like this.

T: Oh, I see. It goes 'way back.

C: Yes. And I have a holster, too.

T: A holster to go with the gun.

C: Doggy, doggy, doggy. (*Puts the dog in the clay and then pulls it out again.*) Woooo. Mmmmmm. Woooo. Little doggy mine.

T: It belongs just to you.

C: These are my sunglasses and my keys.

T: Mm-hm.

C: When the sun's out it's dark and I can't see out of them. I can't.

T: Mm-hm.

C: Sometimes the sun gets in my eyes, so I have to put my sunglasses on.

T: That protects your eyes, doesn't it?

C: Keeps the sun out of my eyes. Gigigigigi. (*Hits comeback toy. Puts it down on the floor and sits on it. Wrestles with it.*) Wooo-wooo-wooo. (*Gets off comeback toy and picks up small nursing bottle.*) Take the nub off. (*Sucks on nipple and pulls nipple off bottle with teeth. Then pours water on the roof of the dollhouse.*) Oooh-oooh.

T: You like doing that, hm?

C: Yes. It's gonna get empty. Wooo-wooo. (*Refills bottle with water and hands nipple to therapist.*) Put it on. (*Replaces small nursing bottle on bench and drinks from large bottle.*) Weee-weee. Mmmm-mmm-mmmm.

T: You like to drink from that bottle.

C: Hmm?

T: You like to drink from that bottle.

C: (*Picks up gun and shoots at therapist.*) Na-na-na-na-na. (*Throws gun into pail of water.*) Mmmm-mmm-mmmm. (*Continues to drink from bottle.*) Aaah-aah. (*Puts down large nursing bottle and picks up small one. Pours water from it on roof of dollhouse.*) It's getting all over the floor. It got on me. I'm gonna go in the bathroom and wipe my pants. O.K.?

T: In here you decide about things for yourself.

C: Well, I'll wipe my pants, 'cause they're wet. (*Returns from bathroom.*) Hmmm. Wooo. Mmmmm. I'll be piggy. I'll get piggy mask. Now no one can see me, can they?

T: No. No one can.

C: (*Replaces mask. Gets small nursing bottle, fills it, and then empties it into toy sink.*) Carry it. Carry it. (*Places some clay in water in toy sink.*) That's to make it soft. (*Returns clay to workbench. Puts small nipple in mouth and chews on it.*) Mmm-mmm. Lookit. That's soft.

T: It's soft now, hm?

C: Yes. See, it's soft. See, it has to be.

T: That's the way you have to do it.

C: (*Takes scissors and cuts clay. Puts small pieces of clay into toy sink.*) Get this soft. Get this soft.

T: It's going to be soft, hm?

C: It's going to be. Wooooo-wooooo. (*Takes dog and buries it in clay.*) Doggy, doggy, doggy gone.

T: Gone away, hm?

C: So nobody will know.

T: You don't want anyone to know.

C: No one knows that he's there, do they?

T: You don't want anybody to know, hm?

C: (*Picks up dog, which is covered with soggy clay, and pushes it toward therapist.*)

T: You want to put it on me, but you may not do that in here. You'd like to, though, wouldn't you?

C: Yes. (*Buries dog in clay again. Cuts big pieces of clay.*) Whole big pieces. Pieces and pieces and pieces. (*Takes dog out of clay.*) Bow. Bow-wow. Bow-wow-wow. (*Pause.*) O.K. I want to go back now.

T: All right. You still have a while left, but if you'd like to leave now, it's up to you.

C: Yes. Let's go.

Discussion: Second Play Session

Joey begins by shooting the gun at the house and later shoots the dog figure. His aggression continues in his attack on the clown.

Feelings of regression are also present in this session. Joey's language is immature at points. He drinks from the nursing bottle and sucks and chews on the nipple. Joey expresses these impulses frequently, evidently gaining considerable release from this behavior. As he expresses these negative attitudes again and again, Joey's feelings become less and less intense and he apparently achieves full satisfaction.

During the third session Joey discarded his baby talk. He did not
return to the nursing bottles. He spent most of his time with the
clay and paints, very freely cutting the clay and soaking it with
paints. He played out his feelings about himself as a boy in a
very unrestrained fashion and was uninhibited in speech and
movements. He made acknowledgment and took responsibility
for his behavior, indicating to the therapist his intentions and
goals.

THIRD PLAY SESSION WITH JOEY

T: You brought your own paper towels today, I see.

C: Yes. (*Walks to the clay and puts pieces of clay on the paper
    towel. Plays with the clay. Cuts it in half and cuts smaller
    pieces.*) See? See what I'm doing?

T: Mm-hm.

C: I have a gun at home. I have a gun at home.

T: You have?

C: Yeah. And it comes down. (*Takes stick and rubs it against
    the vise.*) This goes straight down and makes fur in there.
    It makes fur.

T: Oh, yes.

C: There's a whole bunch of fur on this.

T: An awful lot there.

C: See? See it?

T: Mm-hm.

C: Because some people want fur. This kind of fur.

T: Some people want that kind.

C: Yes. Some people want some of this.

T: Mm-hm.

C: (*Starts molding a piece of clay.*) This is something. It's going
    to be something.

T: It looks like something, hm?

C: Yes. It has to be a little boy.

T: Oh, that's what it has to be.

C: That's why I have to have these two pieces. (*Turns handle of
    vise.*) This one's gonna have some fur on it. (*Points to a
    stick.*)

T: Mm-hm.

C: Already it's got some fur on it. Already. See? It goes round and round. (*Points to the handle of vise.*)

T: Mm-hm.

C: And it gets fur on it. On this side a whole bunch.

T: Mm-hm. A lot of fur there.

C: A whole bunch. Now this is the little boy. (*Leaves clay and walks to the finger paints.*) I have to make it colored.

T: Mm-hm.

C: (*Puts fingers into jars and starts painting on the paper.*) You know, red and blue makes this and this and this. Do you know that it makes purple?

T: I see. You mix those together, you get purple.

C: See?

T: Mm-hm.

C: I need a little water to make it more wet.

T: Mm-hm.

C: Then I can paint it better. (*Smears more paint on the paper.*) Then some yellow. Then some red. Look at it.

T: Just the way you want it.

C: And then you set it down carefully. And then you get some clay and put clay on it. (*Rubs clay across painted paper.*) It's gonna get all painted. All full of paint. There. There. Now I'm gonna get some red and then some yellow. There.

T: Now you've got it.

C: And now I'll mix it all up. Mix it up. Mix it up. This is getting all painted up.

T: Mm-hm.

C: Whole bunches of paint.

T: Mm-hm.

C: (*Scrubs clay onto hands like soap.*) Needs a little more paint. (*Dips hand into paints, which he then squashes onto clay.*) There isn't much left in there.

T: Almost all gone.

C: Lookit! Lookit! It's making purple.

T: Mm-hm.

C: (*Again dips hand into jars of paint and covers clay with paint.*) It looks like polish.

T: Mm-hm.

C: See? You get it all on right over there.

T: Mm-hm.

C: More and more paints over here. (*Takes a big piece of paper and covers clay and paper towel.*) And now we have to let it dry.

T: It has to dry off, hm?

C: (*Cuts clay with scissors and rolls clay in hand.*) This looks like a banana.

T: It looks like a banana, hm?

C: Yes. Bananas cut in half like that.

T: Mm-hm. Split right down the middle.

C: (*Cuts another piece of clay.*) Make some fur, because this has to be a dog.

T: It has to be a dog, so you have to put fur on it.

C: Yes. Dogs need fur. (*Makes a big hole in the clay and inserts dog. Then begins to sing.*) See this? It's deep enough for another dog to go in there. There. That's it. That's better.

T: Mm-hm.

C: That's the way it should go.

T: Mm-hm.

C: (*Continues singing until the end of the play session.*)

Discussion: Third Play Session

In this session Joey proudly makes a little boy, perhaps himself, conveying the attitude that he is ready to play at his own level of maturity. He shows his inner freedom by playing with the finger paints, uninhibited, and using his hands for painting, freely and spontaneously. Whereas in earlier sessions the clay was repeatedly pulled apart into little pieces, it is now used creatively and maturely in the making of friendly dogs with fur.

Following the third play session with Joey a conference was held with the nursery school staff, at which time the nursery school teacher indicated special interest in Joey's use of the nursing bottles and in his baby talk. She stated that she had never seen him use clay as he had in the playroom. His teacher reported that after the first session Joey had exhibited occasional unrestrained outbursts and demands that had not been previously observed.

Within a short period of time, however, these unusual patterns disappeared.

Case materials similar to the recorded data above, as part of the preventive program of mental hygiene, assisted the therapist and the school staff in determining which children were beset with temporarily threatening situations and attitudes and which children were the victims of chronic emotional impoverishment.

All these experiences with normal children gave them an opportunity to have with a member of the adult world a therapeutic relationship, a secure relationship, in and through which the child's life adjustments, including his regressive and aggressive patterns of behavior, were freely expressed and explored in his own way.

CHAPTER IV

Situational Play Therapy [*]

The present chapter is concerned with normal children who were faced with a disturbing new family experience which they perceived as threatening to themselves, and who were given an opportunity to resolve their feelings in situational play therapy sessions. These children who come for situational play therapy ordinarily establish a relationship with the therapist quickly, express their feelings earlier than disturbed children, and are direct in their expressions of attitudes about themselves and others. Therefore children coming for situational play therapy are able to make almost immediate use of the therapeutic situation to express and explore tense and insecure attitudes. Often the threatening emotions are worked out in three or four individual play sessions and one group play session.

In the two cases here described in some detail, both children were faced with one of the commonest crises of childhood, the arrival of a new baby in the family. Of a number of instances in which play therapy sessions were equally effective, these two were selected as providing interesting and clear-cut illustrations of the philosophy.

[*] This chapter is adapted from a paper entitled "Situational Play Therapy with Normal Children," published in the *Journal of Consulting Psychology,* June, 1951. It is reprinted here with permission of the editor, Laurance F. Shaffer.

The New Baby Crisis

Normal children who experience such catastrophes as fires and floods, or who have accidents or illnesses, or who are subjected to such family crises as divorce and death often show confusion, hostility, uncontrollable aggression, hate, and anxiety. The arrival of a new baby in the family is one of the commonest sources of such a disturbance in the child's behavior. To all children such an event brings a period of stress, for however stable, well organized, and rooted in positive emotions the family relationships may be, the arrival of a new family member requires some modification of role in each person in the family. Some family disorganization may result, at least temporarily, and the older child or children may be faced with a difficult adjustment to the new situation.

For neither of the two children, Tommy and Susan, whose play therapy sessions are reported was the arrival of a new baby a surprise. Both had been informed of the coming event two or three months in advance, and both had expressed pleasure in the prospect.

Tommy

Tommy, four years old, had been rated as fairly well adjusted both personally and socially by his nursery school teacher, the nursery school director, and the psychologist. His relations with other nursery school children were satisfactory, he came to school happily, and he talked with pride of his home and parents. His parents, in turn, talked of him with pleasure and pride and regarded him as a happy, secure, confident child who easily accepted limits and responsibilities.

When Tommy was four and a half an adopted girl of thirteen was suddenly brought into the home, and three months later his mother gave birth to a daughter. During this period Tommy's behavior showed a radical change, both at school and at home. At school he became sulky, refused to accept even simple, clear, and reasonable limits, showed a tendency to retreat from child groups whenever things did not go his way, and often withdrew into long sessions of solitary play. At home he became fidgety at mealtimes, refused to eat foods that he had accepted before, cried, attempted to destroy the family record player, and often appeared ill-tempered and irritable. His mother, after attempting to deal with the situation by explanations and supports of many kinds, requested that he be given play therapy.

Three play sessions were conducted with Tommy. During the first he played with airplanes and trucks the entire time and was relatively quiet. In the second session Tommy appeared to focus on his attitudes about himself and what the two new members of the family would mean in terms of his role. He perceived them as potential threats, but once he had recognized these feelings and they had been accepted and clarified, he could accept his siblings and share with them his emotional and material possessions and see his altered role as one that did not threaten his real self. A transcript of this session from the tape recordings follows.

Second Play Session with Tommy

T: You can use these things in any way that you want, Tommy.

C: You know what? I could make a little castle out of that. (*Indicates sand in sandbox.*)

T: You could make a castle.

C: These are two boats. Look.

T: Mm-hm.

C: You know what kind? This one is a ship, and this one is a ferry.

T: One's a ship and one's a ferry.

C: This is the ocean. (*Points to sand.*) This is the way that they use them in New Mexico.

T: In New Mexico they use them like that.

C: Now do you know what we have to do? We have to get some water and smooth it. (*Refers to sand.*) You know what I can do? I can make an ocean liner and put it in the sand.

T: You can do that.

C: Then this can be the dock. (*Points to hill of sand.*) Then the ocean liner can go on it. It can go right on the hill.

T: Mm-hm.

C: There is just room for two boats to be on it. There. Now I'll make another boat. This can be the parking space. (*Points to spot in the sand.*) See? This is a great big parking lot for it.

T: A great big one.

C: See? This is where the little boat goes. He goes way up there. There's a parking lot for the big boat and one for the little boat. We have to do this over at the dock. Toot, toot, toot go the boats. Look where this boat has to go. He goes to get the sand. I'm putting it right in.

T: You're putting it right inside.

C: I'm pretending this is a ship. This is where they really go. Right over here. (*Points to spot in sand.*)

T: That's really the place for them to go.

C: This (*sand*) is the stuff that they carry into the dock. Look what he has to do. He's going to bury this whole big boat.

T: He'll bury the whole big boat.

C: See? I can bury him.

T: You're really burying him.

C: So no one will ever find him again.

T: He will be lost for good.

C: He'll be lost for good. It can't get out now. You see, this is the little boat's dock, and no one ever goes in this dock. Because that's his dock.

T: Just his.

C: You know what he's going to do? He's going to put sand and water on this boat. (*Points to big boat which he has taken out of sand.*) Then he'll clean it up.

T: He'll make it clean.

C: Hi, Joe. Howdy. You see, this big one that comes along is his brother. You see, these two boats are brother boats.

T: One is the brother of the other one.

C: Yeah. One is the brother of the other one. Hey! Who messed my dock up? "Well, I did," says the big boat. See? He has some sand in him. He carries people in his boat, and this one has sand in his, too.

T: They both have sand.

C: You know what? They dump out the sand there. He (*little boat*) scrubs his boat off. Both of them go. You know where they're going now? In the—in the brink the ship goes first (*big boat*). Say, what do you know, Joe? I have to make another dock for this boat (*tiny boat*).

T: Another dock for another boat.

C: Yeah. Oh, I know a nice dock. What do you know, Joe? He'll be lost forever. What do you suppose I'll have to do? Hey! What's the matter with my garage? That's what it will be. What do you know, Joe?

T: What do you know?

C: This is the littlest boat. I have to build so many docks around here.

T: So many docks you have to build.

C: Yes, and all these are brothers. This is the best one (*picks up middle boat*), because, look. He can carry more sand than the other ones.

T: He's the best one of all.

C: You know what? You know what I have to do? See this boat here? That's the littlest one, and this one is the biggest one, and see, those are brothers. These two are brothers, and these two are brothers.

T: They're all brothers.

C. Yes. And they all have some docks, but he (*middle boat*) has the coziest one.

T: He has the nicest, coziest one.

C: And this (*big boat*) and this (*little boat*) each have one, but he (*middle boat*) can carry nice soft dirt for people to the lake. We better not use this boat (*tiny boat*). You know, this is the guy who stands and has to watch all of these things. (*Picks up policeman figure and gestures toward boats.*) And this one. You know what? I'm pretending that this is an oil place, and that's where the boats get their power. You know, they don't have any power when they start off. They come around, and after awhile they put their boats in this place where they can get power.

T: That's what they do.

C: I know what I'm doing. You know what I'm pretending? This is all the family, the whole family, the whole family. This is the family.

T: You're pretending it's the whole family.

C: Yeah. I have to. Well, what do you know? What do you know, Joe? What do you know, Joe? Linga, linga, linga, linga, linga, linga. Hey! I'm pretending. You see these cowboys? They're the guards.

T: They are the guards, huh?

C: All of them. They're the guards of these garages.

T: They guard them.

C: They guard them. There's the guard. You see, if anyone comes around to steal the boats—well, they'll shoot them.

T: They shoot anyone who tries to steal the boats.

C: There's another guard. He's a husky one. Look, there's sand in this boat (*middle one*). He carries it well. Golly, he's stuck in a ditch, but he's cozy. Cozy, but him and him—no, really every three of them are the coziest.

T: Every three of them.

C: This is the best cowboy, and he guards this boat (*middle boat*). Linga, linga, linga. You know what? They watch to see that no one steals anything. They watch the garages, too. One guard in front of each garage.

T: One in front of each garage.

C: See, these are very lucky, because they have guards. They're very lucky.

T: Very, very lucky, because they have guards.

C: No one else has guards but them.

T: No one but them.

C: This guard watches this (*big boat*). This guard watches this (*middle boat*). And this guards this one (*tiny boat*). This guy (*middle boat*) is lucky. He's lucky because he has the nicest house, the nicest house of all. He has the best house of all. He can just fit in right well. These (*the other two boats*) are lucky, too. They have power. They squeeze right in. He has power, too. He goes over and gets his power.

T: You have just a short while longer to play.

C: There he goes. See? He goes to his brother's place.

T: He's going right to his brother's place.

C: Hey, ring, ring! It's me. I'm your brother. It's all right. I was here before you, but come with me. Hey! Big boat and little boat say, "Please give me some power," and middle boat says, "O.K." Middle boat: "I'm going to get more power. Hey, Joe. Come on. I'll help you. We've got the best house in the world. We'll get some power. All we'll have to do is back right out and get it. We can get our power and gas easy." Linga, linga, linga. We can go now. When others come in, they'll be able to see that I built all this.

T: They'll see it right there where you built it.

Discussion: Second Play Session

In this relationship Tommy approaches, step by step, his difficulties in being suddenly confronted with two new family members. Tommy feels that his status in the family is precarious. He uses boats to represent his two new siblings and himself and steadily approaches his home situation. In his play he first builds a dock and an ocean for the ships. Next he makes a parking lot with spaces for the two boats which represent his sisters. Tommy uses a policeman to protect his possessions and make sure that his own boat is the nicest boat, the coziest boat, the best boat of all. The parking lots become garages and are eventually symbolized as a home. In the end the boats become "brother boats," and Tommy shares his "power" with his siblings. He indicates that "we've got the best house in the world," describing his feelings of happiness and security in his family.

The therapeutic process for Tommy included three stages: (1) negative feelings toward his new siblings expressed again and again with considerable feeling, (2) ambivalent feelings, less intense, and (3) positive feelings toward his siblings and a willingness to share some of his belongings, including his home.

After the third play session, which was similar to the second, Tommy said he felt that he would not have to come back any more. He then went to his mother, she reported, and said, "Look here, Mother. There are some things that are mine, really mine. They belong just to me, and there are other things that I can share and will gladly share." His mother responded, "Of course, Tommy. That's the way it will always be."

The nursery school staff and Tommy's parents reported that

Tommy had once again become the affable, free, expressive child they had known before.

SUSAN

The nursery school staff described Susan, three years old, as a charming youngster whose winning smile and understanding ways had made her popular with both children and adults. Her mother had considered Susan's relations with her parents and an older sibling excellent. When Susan was three years and three months a new baby arrived in the family. Two days after the mother and the new baby daughter arrived home Susan became babyish, immature, and whining at home. This behavior became evident in the nursery school as well. Susan's mother frantically telephoned the nursery school one day to ask whether something could be done to stop Susan's constant whining, which had annoyed everyone in the family. She could not understand how so wonderful and confident a child could have become a whimpering, clinging one in so short a time.

The nursery school staff referred Susan to the play therapist, who conducted three play sessions with her. During the first two sessions Susan appeared to project her negative and hostile feelings for the new baby onto the humanlike balloon figure in the therapy room, throwing it on the floor, stepping on it, squeezing its head and face, and crushing it inside the vise. Once her feelings were recognized, accepted, and at least partly clarified, she proceeded in the last session to pick up the balloon figure, kiss it, toss it in the air, and dance around the room while she held it in her arms.

A transcript of recordings of the three sessions follows.

FIRST PLAY SESSION WITH SUSAN

(*Mother and child walk into the room together.*)
Therapist: You can use these in any way you like.
(*Mother starts to leave room, and child looks at her.*)
CHILD: No, you stay here for awhile.
MOTHER: Watch the watch. When this hand gets over here, I'll be
    back.
C: O.K. I'll bounce two balls.

T: Two at a time you did.

M: I'll lay down the watch where you can watch it.

C: O.K. It's not ticking.

M: Want me to put it on you? (*Places watch on C's wrist.*) Bye. You can just keep your eye on that watch.

C: (*Waves good-by to mother.*) Where's the baby?

T: Where do you suppose the baby could be?

C: Here? That's the baby. Lookit the big baby. This is a balloon head. Mr. Balloon Head. (*Picks up a balloon in the form of a human figure. Squeezes balloon and cries, "Mommy, mommy, mommy."*)

T: That's what it cries. Mommy, mommy, mommy.

C: (*Continues to squeeze balloon and cry "Mommy, mommy, mommy." Looks at T and places balloon on table. Turns handle of vise.*) What is it?

T: You want to know what it could be. It can be anything you want it to be.

C: A can opener.

T: Is that what it is? A can opener?

C: Lookit these soldiers. Are these cowboys or soldiers?

T: What do they look like?

C: Cowboys. See the cowboys. Those are all cowboys.

T: Mm-hm.

C: I'm gonna be a monkey.

T: That's what you're going to be.

C: (*Puts on monkey mask.*) Lookit me. I'm the monkey.

T: Susan is the monkey.

C: Now I'm gonna be a piggy. I'll say oink, oink. (*Puts on pig mask.*) Oink, oink, oink, oink, oink.

T: The piggy goes oink, oink, oink.

C: Oink, oink, oink, oink. (*Takes mask off.*) Now I'm gonna be a clown. This goes oink, oink, oink, too. Oink, oink.

T: The clown goes oink, oink.

C: Oink, oink, oink. (*Laughs.*) Now I'm gonna be a baby and drink from the bottle of water. Shall I?

T: That's up to you.

C: Should I sprinkle here? Here. Open your hand.

T: You want to sprinkle in my hand.

C: (*Sprinkles water in T's hand.*) Rub them together. (*Drinks from bottle and then replaces it on bench. Turns handle of vise again.*) Now I have to can-opener this. (*Puts figure balloon into vise; it squeaks.*) She doesn't want to be can-openered.

T: She doesn't?

C: No. I heard my mummy walking. Hey! It's almost up to here. This number right there. (*Indicates number on wrist watch.*) I hear her coming.

T: You hear her coming.

C: (*Turns handle of vise. Shakes it back and forth. Looks at nursing bottles. Again turns vise handle and looks out window. Picks up figure balloon and squeezes it; drops it and steps on it.*) I'm gonna throw the ball. You kick it like that.

T: Mm-hm. That's what you do to it.

C: See what you do? Rocky-rocky the baby to sleep. Where's the baby? Where is she? Here's a mirror.

T: Mm-hm.

C: (*Peers in mirror of dresser.*) Tick-tick.

T: That's the way it goes.

C: Tick-tock. Tick-tock. There's the baby in there. (*Points to doll-house.*) Baby walking upstairs. One, two, three, four, five. Into your beds. They're in their beds. Into your bed you go, bad girl. (*Baby doll.*) And this one is a big girl.

T: A big girl.

C: With a round head. Walk, walk, walk. Here's the daddy going to bed now. Walky, walky, walky. Right next to the girl. (*Middle doll.*)

T: Mm-hm.

C: And here's the mommy. Walky, walky, walky. Right next to the baby. (*Undresses male doll.*) I'm taking his pantsies off.

T: Mm-hm. You're taking his pants off.

C: Walk, walk, walk. Walking up to bed, walking up to bed. Three little children.

T: Three little children and two big people.

C: And another little baby. Here's me. I'm taking her clothes off. I'm going to bed. Now he's up. (*Male doll.*) Up and up and up. (*Dressing male doll.*) Little up, little up. Put your pants back on. Walky, walky, walky downstairs. (*Female doll.*) Walky, walky, walky downstairs. (*Male doll.*) Walky, walky, walky. (*Another male doll. Walks baby doll downstairs.*) I'm climbing up this ladder. Let's climb up the ladders. Just climbing up the ladders.

T: Mm-hm.

C: And the little one on top of the bed. (*Middle doll.*) The little one sleeps under the bed. (*Baby doll.*)

T: One on top, one underneath.

C: Two underneath. Here's the bedroom. (*Bends figure balloon and squeezes it.*) I like that noise. Squeak, squeak, squeak. This is a big bed. Here's your bed.

T: That's my bed, huh?

C: Who sleeps in that *bed?*

T: Anyone you want.

C: Me. This is my little chair. (*Crouches and sits on bed.*) How come this doesn't go? (*Points to watch on arm.*)

T: You wonder why it doesn't go.

C: Oh. Supper is open. Here's your supper.

T: Quite a supper.

C: That's my mother's watch. Just pretend it's your supper. (*Turns handle of vise.*) Zoom, zoom, zoom, zoom. Here's your supper. Eat it up. Don't eat my mother's watch up. Just eat your supper up. Zoom, zoom, zoom. Here's your watch. Zoom, zoom, zoom. Here's your watch.

Discussion: First Session

Immediately in this session Susan asks for the baby. The therapeutic process begins with Susan unleashing terrific feelings against her baby sister. Susan's feelings are very clearly focused. She squeezes the balloon and mimics the baby, resentfully. The hostility continues with an attempt to crush the baby's head in the vise. Then Susan expresses a desire to "can-opener" the balloon figure representing her sister. Later she drinks from the baby bottle, indicating perhaps a strong interest in being the baby herself and being immature. Susan succeeds in her wish to "can-opener" the baby, while recognizing that the baby doesn't want to be "can-openered." At this point Susan shows a little anxiety.

She crushes the baby balloon figure in the vise, steps back, appears frightened, and imagines her mother approaching. Calm again, Susan repeatedly attacks the baby balloon figure, squeezing it, dropping it, and throwing and kicking it. The hostility continues as Susan throws the baby doll under the bed and indicates it is the place for the baby to sleep. She places herself between the mother and father, showing she wants to have the favorite place.

SECOND PLAY SESSION WITH SUSAN

C: (*Talks to mother.*) Are you gonna stay here? Here's a balloon. (*Waves a balloon figure at T.*) Good-by (*to mother*). Mommy, leave your watch here. I want to see what time it is. (*Looks at T's watch.*) It will still be there tomorrow. (*Puts balloon figure in upper part of dollhouse. Empties bag of dolls.*) There. In the garbage can. (*Walks to nursing bottles.*) I'm gonna drink from this. (*Drinks from large bottle and replaces it on bench.*) He's gonna shoot you. (*Cowboy figure.*) Bang. Hoppy is gonna shoot you. Shoot you and tie you up. All cowboys are shooting. (*Handles soldiers and shoots T a few times.*) Everyone is shot. (*Squeezes figure balloon and it squeaks. Walks figure balloon up the stairs of dollhouse.*) Walk, walk, walk. (*Throws figure balloon aside. Sits on floor, fingers stairway. Picks up figure balloon and whispers.*) She's going to sleep. Shall I take her head off?

T: That's up to you.

C: (*Places balloon in box with blocks.*) That's a block. (*Picks up figure balloon again, brushes it against T's face.*) I wanta take your glasses off.

T: You'd like to do that, but that's one thing you can't do here.

C: Let's pretend to play school. O.K.? And you're the teacher. O.K.?

T: And I'm the teacher.

C: (*Cuts a piece of paper and folds it in half. Cuts paper along folded line and into quarters. Looks at T, folds paper again and shows it to T.*) I'm gonna give these to my mother. That's for Mother's Day.

T: Is that a Mother's Day present?

C: Yeah. (*Cuts another piece of paper in two.*) This is my mother's present, too.

T: You have quite a few to give your mother. You like to give her things, huh?

C: (*Holds papers in hand.*) These are my mother's and my daddy's, too. Just for my mother and daddy. (*Lifts comeback toy.*) He's a big clown.

T: Mm-hm.

C: (*Carries comeback toy to T.*) There. Walk, walk, walk, walk, walk.

T: There you go.

C: (*Leans against comeback toy, pushing it down.*)

T: You want it to go down.

C: Yeah. (*Pushes comeback toy into sandbox.*) He's crying.

T: You're making him cry.

C: Yeah. (*Finally succeeds in pushing comeback toy into sandbox.*)

T: There, you have it.

C: He's crying. Nobody's taking him out.

T: He is just going to stay in there all the time.

C: (*Hands T papers that she has cut.*) Will you fold these for my mother? And my dad.

T: For no one else.

C: Not even you.

T: Not even me.

C: No. (*Starts to cut paper again. Continues. Folds one half-sheet in two again and places it on top of the others.*) See? Some's for my family, and not for you, either.

T: Not for me.

C: No. (*Cuts more paper.*) Only one is for you, and this is all you're getting. Here. None for your mother. No. It's all mine and my mother's.

T: Just yours and your mother's.

C: I'll be the teacher and gather up your things. O.K., honey. Let's, honey. Yes, honey. Where's that paper? And you, honey. Honey, honey. I'm gonna sprinkle some. (*Drops a handful of sand from sandbox into pail of water. Watches it.*

Takes more sand and drops it into pail. Looks at T and laughs.) It's all getting brown, isn't it? (*Throws more sand into pail.*) The floor is getting wet. (*Continues. to drop handfuls of sand into pail.*) It's getting brown water.

T: Yes, it is. It's getting to be brown water.

C: (*Throws more sand into pail.*) I splashed my shoe. See? (*Sprinkles some sand over comeback toy. Drops more sand into pail and waves her hands in the air.*) I wanta go wash them.

T: You want to go wash them? O.K.

C: (*Leaves room with T.*)

Discussion: Second Play Session

Susan begins this session with an expression of hostility against the entire family, throwing the family doll figures in the garbage can. Feeling free, Susan regresses and drinks from the large nursing bottle. She eliminates the therapist by having cowboys shoot him and tie him up. Susan returns to the object of her strongest negative feelings, her baby sister. She squeezes and squeeks the baby balloon figure and fluctuates between pulling off her head and putting her to sleep, perhaps permanently.

Another level of the therapeutic process begins. Susan expresses positive feelings for her mother and father, making them presents. She shows mixed emotions toward the therapist, telling him there will be no presents for him or his mother and then calling him "honey" a number of times. Though unclearly expressed, there appear to be some positive feelings for the baby as Susan decides to give presents to "my family."

At the end of the session Susan regresses in her play. She drops handfuls of sand in the water and delights in hearing the sound and seeing the brown color. Susan seems relaxed and satisfied as the session ends.

THIRD PLAY SESSION WITH SUSAN

C: (*Waves good-by to mother and runs into the room. Drops a handful of sand into pail of water.*)

T: It went right in, didn't it?

C: Look how much. (*Drops another, larger handful into pail and laughs.*) A big splash. Splash. The water's getting brown. (*Drops two more handfuls of sand into the pail.*)

T: It's getting browner and browner.

C: Mmm. Now I'm making pie. (*Plays in sandbox.*)

T: So you're making a pie, that's what.

C: Here's your pie.

T: Is that for me?

C: Mmm. Take a shovel and eat it. Take a spoon and eat it.

T: You want me to eat it.

C: (*Throws more sand into pail and smiles at T.*) O.K. Here. (*Gestures toward T with shovel.*)

T: You want me to eat with that, huh?

C: Not really.

T: You just want me to pretend?

C: Yes.

T: Mm-hm.

C: I'm throwing it all over the floor. (*Throws sand on the floor.*)

T: You are?

C: Swoosh, swoosh, swoosh.

T: You really like that.

C: (*Continues to play with sand.*) Now this is a little cookie, and I'll put it in a plate.

T: Mm-hm.

C: Here. And I'll give you some more. (*Throws more sand into pail.*) It's getting dark blue.

T: That's what it's getting to be. Dark blue.

C: (*Fills mold with sand, pats it, and gives it to T.*) Eat it.

T: You want me to eat it now.

C: And then I'll give you some more. Eat it up. O.K. Now eat it.

T: Now you want me to eat it. Suppose that I don't want any more?

C: Then you won't get any dessert. Now eat it all up. O.K., now take it. Now pick it up now. Hello, hello, hello, hello. (*Dials telephone.*) Pretend I hear the phone bell ringing, and I say "Hello," and you talk.

T: Oh, all right. We'll pretend that.

C: Hello?

T: Hello.

C: Who is this?

T: Who is that?

C: This is Susan, and she's playing here. Good-by.

T: Good-by. (*Sneezes.*)

C: God bless you.

T: Thank you.

C: (*Picks up large bottle and drinks. Replaces it on bench.*) I like to play here.

T: You like coming here and playing.

C: (*Walks over to balloon figure and kisses it. Tosses it into air and catches it several times while dancing around the room.*)

T: Well, our time is up for today, Susan.

C: One more bouncy and I'll go up.

T: O.K., one more bouncy and we'll go.

C: (*Throws balloon figure into air one more time. Lets it fall on floor.*) O.K. Good-by, good-by. Good-by, Mister.

T: Good-by.

Discussion: Third Play Session

Susan continues her immature play, dropping sand in water and enjoying the browner and browner color of the water. A third level of the therapeutic process has begun. Susan's feelings are not only more moderate but are also more positive. She wants to share her "pie" with the therapist. Later she gives him his supper and tells him, perhaps reflecting the family situation, that unless he eats it up he won't get any dessert.

Susan's feelings toward her baby sister are now positive in her play. She takes the baby balloon figure, kisses it, tosses it into the air, and dances around the room.

For Susan the basic aspects of the process may be summarized as follows: (1) direct hostility toward the baby with strong accompanying feelings, (2) ambivalence in her feelings toward the baby, unclearly expressed, and (3) positive feelings and interest in her baby sister.

Susan's mother came in after this last session to tell the therapist that she was happy about Susan, who had again become a pleasant child; that she was no longer afraid to leave Susan with the baby;

that Susan showed more affection for the baby and had assumed some responsibilities in the baby's care.

BENEFITS OF PLAY THERAPY FOR THESE
TWO CHILDREN

Both Tommy and Susan used symbolic forms—boats and balloon figures—to localize their anxiety about a new baby in the family. The gains in both cases were growth in terms of emotional insight, a feeling of security and comfort within themselves. What they needed was an opportunity to express their negative attitudes in an accepting relationship where they felt that the therapist had faith in them and respected them as individuals, whatever their feelings and perceptions about themselves and their families might be.

Situational play therapy provided these children with an opportunity to work out temporarily disturbing feelings and so removed the possibility that these feelings would be repressed, lose their identification with reality, become distorted, and perhaps eventually seriously damage the child. Freed from these temporarily disturbing feelings, these children were able to use their energy more effectively in both personal and social situations with other children and adults.

CHAPTER V

Play Therapy with Disturbed Children

Dorie is a disturbed child with two distinctive moods. She presents contrasting emotional patterns that struggle for supremacy. The moods alternate in enveloping her. Sometimes she is restless and nervous, moving about and talking, unable to concentrate, to work, or to play. At other times she is quiet, almost motionless, laboring for long periods over a single problem or task. As she jumps from one activity to another, she may be heard shouting over and over again, "What'll I do first? What'll I do first?" She can be completely oblivious to the world of children and adults around her, not hearing, not responding. Other people see her as a funny child, jerky, peculiar, and bizarre in her mannerisms and behavior.

Disturbed children like Dorie are immobilized personally and socially, responding in inhibited, unnatural ways. They are sometimes seen by their teachers as uncontrollable, wildly aggressive, cruel, demanding, and moody. During other periods they are perceived as anxious, frightened, painfully silent, often withdrawing from other children and adults.

Some disturbed children spend their time in solitary play. Others continually bicker and fight. Many of them cannot make decisions or assume responsibilities. Parents often describe disturbed children as selfish, mean, stubborn, inconsiderate, difficult to handle.

They complain, too, that their children cannot be taught, that they do not seem to want to learn respect and consideration.

The disturbed child, in a sense, is caught in a restricted circle. He sees himself as an inferior person, unloved, inadequate, and afraid of the consequences of his behavior. He is threatened by criticism and punishment. Nor do reward and approval have a constructive effect. Reward and approval are perceived as attempts to change or modify him, and, however inadequate he may feel, he will struggle to maintain his own picture of himself in spite of all allurements. Punishment and disapproval, on the other hand, are reminders, mirrors of the child's own inadequacies, which reinforce his own feelings of insecurity and sometimes terrify him. He is so afraid to make new responses that he continues to operate within the safe and familiar patterns of his life.

Child-centered play therapy does not offer reward and approval, nor does it extol punishment and criticism. The therapist is not involved in thoughts about modifying the child or in ways of pressuring the child to change. He approaches the child with a sincere feeling of belief in the child as a person who has capacities for working out his difficulties. He respects the child entirely, not merely his momentary kindnesses, expressions of good will, gentleness, and politeness, but also his fears and hatreds and resentments. The disturbed child often views the relationship with the therapist as quite different from any other he has known.

Disturbed children use the therapeutic relationship in diverse ways. They express and explore underlying attitudes which in the past have seemed too threatening to reveal. Only when they are completely accepted can they do this. Then they can express themselves fully without feeling ashamed and guilty. They project these feelings and attitudes through media such as paints, clay, sand, and water, using these materials symbolically, giving them personal meanings. In the process they learn to make decisions and to act more spontaneously and confidently. They use the relationship and the media in gradual attempts to grow within themselves and to gain a more realistic impression of themselves.

Some children may remain completely silent in their first few play sessions. They speak only with great difficulty to the therapist. Their initial reactions are made cautiously and deliberately. They use a small area in the room and a few toys. They often want to be told what to do and what not to do. Other children may keep up a rapid-fire flow of questions and conversation during their early sessions. They are often aggressive and want to destroy the play materials, and sometimes they want to destroy the therapist. Richard, a seven-year-old boy, screamed out during his third play session,

C: I'll drill the whole place full of lead! Do you hear me? I'm gonna dirty this place up so far that I don't think you'll be able to clean this stuff up with all the water in the world. I'm gonna really fix this stuff, I'm telling you. I'm gonna mess this room up like a coyote. And then I'll take this jack-knife and cut everything up. Then I'll try it on you next!

T: You want to show me how very angry you can be.

C: And, by George, I am angry! And nobody will be able to clean this darn place up ever again!

Whether seemingly passive or stormy, it is through individual ways of reacting to the situation and to the therapist that each child works through his attitudes and reorganizes them, so that he has a better understanding of himself as a person in the world of reality in which he lives.

LINDA

Linda, four years old, an only child, was considered seriously maladjusted by her nursery school teacher and the school psychologist. In school she showed two clear-cut patterns of behavior. Often Linda remained completely by herself, sitting and staring at the toys, only occasionally reaching out to handle them. At other times Linda was socially aggressive, in a destructive way, attacking other children and interfering with their play. She had no friends in school. She was rarely seen with other children, and most of her contacts at school were with adults. Frequently these contacts were characterized by whining behavior. Her nursery school teacher had considerable difficulty with Linda and described her as a moody, unpredictable child. The mother bitterly described Linda as an obstinate, willful, destructive child at home and a frightened, retiring child away from home. The mother looked upon play therapy pessimistically and despaired of any approach to Linda being gainful.

The background data available on the family relationships included the mother's exaggerated emphasis on cleanliness from Linda's babyhood, the parents' feelings that Linda would never realize their expectations, the parents' frequent threats to Linda for "bad" behavior, the parents' belief that Linda had always been a passive and withdrawn child without much spark, and the parents' regular bitter quarrels in Linda's presence.

Linda first came in contact with the play therapist as part of her scheduled play sessions in conjunction with the nursery school program. The nature of these play sessions motivated a conference between the nursery school staff and the play therapist, at which time it was recommended that Linda be seen regularly by the play therapist. Linda herself had asked to return after her final scheduled play experience.

Linda had eight consecutive individual play therapy experiences. Then her mother abruptly and without explanation began to bring Linda very irregularly. During her experiences in the playroom, Linda apparently changed her attitudes to some degree toward herself and others. At first she was a frightened, restricted child, insecure and indecisive, who played in mutelike silence. Later she became talkative, decisive, and spontaneous in her play. She also became quite aggressive and sometimes demanding in her relationship with the therapist.

Although the therapist did not feel that Linda had completely worked out her tremendous hostility toward people, he felt that she had come a long way in expressing and exploring these hostile attitudes. Five of Linda's play therapy sessions have been selected for presentation.

First Play Session with Linda

During Linda's first session she remained completely silent. She seemed to be frightened and suspicious of the situation and the therapist. She approached the materials cautiously and confined her play to a few toys, which she used in a small space, and to doll furniture, which she crammed into one room of a large doll house.

Linda entered the playroom and walked to a small table with

numerous toys. She stood almost motionless, staring at the toys for a few minutes. The therapist could detect no feeling, no expression whatever on her face. Apathetically she picked up a small truck and looked at it for quite a while. She then lined up a few trucks, made a circle of them and crammed into this small space an airplane, a truck, and a boat. On top of these toys she placed a large gun. Then she quickly stepped away from the table and just stood staring at what she had done. During the following ten minutes Linda arranged every object on the table in orderly rows. After this she built up three high columns, setting one toy on top of another.

Once again she moved away from the table and stared at the toys for quite some time. Then she glanced quickly around the room and for a few seconds focused her attention on the dollhouse and furniture. She moved lethargically toward the house. She looked at the doll figures, picked them up, and undressed them very slowly. Then she put each of them under a bed. Linda spent the remainder of the first session forcing every piece of doll furniture into one small room of the dollhouse. She remained silent throughout the session and did not look at the therapist.

SECOND PLAY SESSION WITH LINDA

This session began where the first had ended. Linda walked slowly to the dollhouse, knelt, and began placing furniture in it. This time she used two rooms of the house. When she had difficulty fitting some pieces of furniture into the rooms, she would put them on top of other pieces, until the two rooms looked like huge masses of furniture. Linda then undressed each of the doll figures. She pulled off the head of a large male doll, looked at the detached body for a while, and then replaced the head. She shoved all the dolls together on two beds.

Toward the end of the session Linda took some furniture from the two crowded rooms and placed it on the floor. She dressed each doll and placed them face down on the floor. Once again Linda was completely silent during this session.

THIRD PLAY SESSION WITH LINDA

In the third play session Linda shifted radically to a new pattern of behavior. She talked throughout the entire session. In the first half she wanted to be told what to do. She repeatedly asked for reassurance and often asked for help. Later in the session she made decisions of her own and carried them out. She approached her reported phobia of knives by examining them, asking about them, and then using them in her play. She clearly showed her hostility toward people as she expressed a desire to bathe the dolls in red paint: "I'll put some people in there, and then they'll get all red. They'll be red all over." Linda, however, did not carry out this threat. Instead she transferred anger to water play, throwing water all over the floor, stamping around in it, and screaming.

C: (*Enters and carefully examines room. Walks to work bench and points to jars of finger paints.*) What is this?
T: What do you suppose?
C: (*Very softly.*) I don't know.
T: You just don't know what's in there.
C: Paint. (*Tries to open a jar of paint, then hands it to therapist.*) Open this.
T: It's kind of hard to do, isn't it?
C: What is it?
T: What does it look like to you?
C: I don't know. What do we use it for?
T: Well, you can use it in any way you want.
C: (*Opens all three jars of paint and then dumps a box of crayons on work bench.*) Crayons. There's a green and white and brown and yellow.
T: All different colors, hm?
C: This is pink.
T: Mm-hm.
C: That one's brown.
T: Mm-hm.
C: They fell out.
T: Mm-hm.

C: (*Points to rubber knives.*) Can I paint those that are down there?

T: In here, Linda, you do whatever you like. You decide for yourself.

C: (*Picks up a rubber knife.*) Well, what is this?

T: What could it be, Linda?

C: I don't know. (*Pause.*) A knife. It's a knife.

T: That's what it is, hm? A knife.

C: (*Points to knife sheath.*) Why can it come out of here for?

T: Why do you suppose?

C: I know why. It's to use it. Could I—? (*Pause.*) Could I take it home?

T: You want to take it home, Linda, I know, but I can't let anything go out of the playroom.

C: Why?

T: Why do you suppose?

C: No child could play with it then. (*Picks up small toy table.*) Can I paint this?

T: You can do whatever you like here. It's up to you.

C: I *want* to paint it.

T: That's what you want to do, hm?

C: How do you paint with this stuff?

T: That's difficult to figure out, isn't it?

C: (*Looks at paints for a long while and then picks up a clown mask.*) What kind of face could that be?

T: You wonder about that.

C: What is it? It's a silly face.

T: Silly as it could be.

C: (*Points to a pig mask.*) What is this one?

T: That one's an odd one, isn't it?

C: Like a pig's. (*Indicates the monkey mask.*) All of them look the same. This one looks like a man. Oh, it's funny. Ha, ha, ha.

T: Really funny, and it looks like a man, hm?

C: (*Drops the mask and returns to table. Picks up scissors.*) Can I cut this paper here?

T: That's up to you, Linda.

C: I'm gonna cut it off right here.

T: Mm-hm.

C: I want to paint something. I want to paint something.

T: You'd like to paint a little something.

C: I don't want to paint it with my hands.

T: You want to do it with something, but not your hands, hm?

C: I want to do it with something. Can you give me anything to do it with?

T: What would you suggest?

C: (*Starts cutting small pieces from edge of paper.*) What was that?

T: That was only the people upstairs talking and moving around.

C: What were they making that noise for?

T: I think they were on their way out of the building.

C: (*Holds up a piece of paper.*) You make me a Christmas tree.

T: In here you do things for yourself, Linda.

C: How could you make it?

T: How do you suppose we might do it?

C: Well, you fold it this way. What's in that door over there?

T: Oh, that's just a storage room.

C: I want to go in there and see.

T: You want to go in the room and see. Well, that room is locked. There's no way of getting into it unless you have a key.

C: Why don't you have a key? Will you help me finish this Christmas tree?

T: What would you like me to do, Linda?

C: You could draw it on there, and I'll cut it.

T: Well, you'll have to show me how to do it. Where shall I begin?

C: Well, it goes like this. All the way from here up to here. (*Outlines the tree on the paper.*) Now it looks like a Christmas tree.

T: It does. Just like a Christmas tree.

C: It goes in and out, in and out on two sides. (*Cuts out the tree and places it on the table. Looks at paints.*) I don't want to put it on with my hands.

T: You can use whatever you want here, Linda.

C: Could I use a crayon?

T: That's up to you, Linda.

C: I could put some paint on here and then put it on the paper. (*Dips crayon into paint jar and smears the paint on paper. Then points to Christmas tree.*) It's sticky. Now I'll paint this.

T: Mm-hm.

C: There. Now I can close it up here and paint it up to there. (*Picks up pieces of furniture and paints them. Takes a toy table and paints it red.*) Now look what kind it is.

T: What kind is it now?

C: You guess.

T: Let's see, what might it be?

C: Red. It's red. (*Smears yellow paint over red paint.*) Now it's yellow. And now it's blue. The next child to come over—. What will you have for her?

T: You tell me, Linda.

C: Just the same things. Just what's here now. Now the next time I'm gonna paint up the window.

T: That's what you'll do, hm?

C: (*Picks up toy dressing table and paints the mirror.*) It's painted red. (*Paints the bathtub with red paint.*) It's red all over. Drown them.

T: You want to drown them?

C: I'll put them in there and get them all red. They'll be red all over.

T: You'd like to see them get all red.

C: (*Points to bathtub.*) In here. In here. That's where to put them.

T: That's just where you want to put them, in the red paints.

C: All red. All red. And I'm gonna do it now.

T: You'll put them in right now.

C: (*Stares at the doll figures for a few seconds.*) I'm gonna go wash my hands. I can turn the light on by myself.

T: O.K. You only have a few minutes left, Linda, and then we'll have to stop for today.

C: (*Returns from bathroom.*) How come there are two knives here?

T: For whatever you want to use them.

C: I'd like to take one home and leave the other one here.

T: Well, you can't take anything out of the playroom, Linda.

C: I'm gonna put one around me and buckle it. (*Puts both knives around her waist. Then holds one knife in each hand and pushes balloons around the room, first with one knife and then with the other, making wild motions. Suddenly runs to large nursing bottle and pours water on the floor. Empties pail of water on floor. Runs into bathroom to get another pailful of water and overturns this on the floor. Laughs very hard and stamps around in the water as the play session ends, yelling unintelligibly and screaming angrily at everything in the room.*)

Discussion: Play Sessions One through Three

Linda begins by expressing anxious behavior. Her fears are vague and unclear. They are without focus. She appears reluctant to use the toys and is suspicious. She seems to act devoid of feelings, and yet there is a deep tenseness about her. She continues in a restrictive, fearful way for quite some time and only gradually expands her relationship with the therapist and the materials. The therapist accepts Linda's silence and does not in any way pressure her into verbalizing her feelings.

In the third session Linda shows anxiety in her repeated questions, most of which are not information questions. She seeks support continually from the therapist. She uses diverse strategies to get the therapist to do things for her. She attempts to avoid making decisions and taking the responsibility for her behavior. The therapist tries to show her that he understands and accepts her feelings, while at the same time he encourages Linda to make decisions for herself and to do whatever she wants to do.

Linda pretends at first not to recognize the rubber knife in the playroom. (Her mother had reported that she had a tremendous fear of knives.) Linda later expresses a desire to take the knife home. This is Linda's first attempt in the play situation to come to grips with her fear of knives.

Linda's anxiety returns as she struggles to decide whether or not she should paint and how she should paint. She still approaches the items in the room cautiously and tentatively. Her insecurity is expressed many times in her attempts to get the therapist to make decisions for her.

Toward the end of the session Linda decides to paint. Now her behavior seems to show why it has been so difficult for her to get started. Behind her diffuse fears there are strong feelings of anger. Once she starts painting Linda becomes hostile, in a generalized way, as she paints various pieces of the doll furniture with red paints. Then, more directly, she expresses a desire to drown "them," the family doll figures, in the red-painted and soaked bathtub. Unable to carry out this desire, Linda shows diffuse anger, spilling water on the floor, stamping around in it, and swinging two rubber knives around the room.

Sixth Play Session with Linda

In the sixth session Linda continued to show growth in her ability to make decisions and to act spontaneously. She showed much more confidence in her play, frequently saying "Because I wanted to" as an explanation for her behavior. She engaged in a vacillating battle between the expression of hostility against people and a desire to be constructive in her play. Apparently in this session Linda progressed further in working out her fear of knives. At first she fearfully threatened to cut the therapist with the rubber knives. Later she unconcernedly ran the blades across her hands.

C: (*Runs into the room and goes immediately to the pail of water, shouting.*) I'll throw it right on the floor! I'll put it right on the rug! (*Spills water on the floor.*) So there. So there.

T: It went all over the floor, and some went near the rug.

C: Yes.

T: You like to spill it over, hm?

C: I'd like to stomp it all over your face.

T: You'd like to stomp it on me, but that's one of the things you may not do in here.

C: (*Walks to the vise and touches it.*) Open this for me. I can't do it.

T: You can't do it, hm?

C: Nope.

T: (*Opens the vise.*)

C: I teased you. Goody, goody, goody.

T: You teased me, hm? You could have done it all the time.

C: (*Laughs.*) You found out.

T: Mm-hm.

C: I'll stomp you with this.

T: You really want to stomp the water on me, but I cannot let you do that.

C: Why?

T: You just may not do that here.

C: (*Laughs loudly.*) Then I'll stomp in it, and I don't care if I get all wet. Hey! My sock is wet. I'm gonna throw some more water on the floor. (*Takes pail into bathroom and enters with it filled with water.*) I'm gonna spill it all over.

T: There, it splattered all over.

C: (*Laughs.*) Let 'er splatter all over. Lock the door. Lock it for me.

T: You want the door to be locked, hm?

C: Yes. You do it for me. No one can get in here. I'll splash them if they try.

T: You want us to be here alone.

C: (*Steps around in puddles of water. Then goes to dollhouse.*) I'm gonna move the house. I'm gonna put it right in the water.

T: Right in the middle of the water, hm?

C: Yes. I'm gonna put it in the water. And if somebody comes up this chimney, they'll put the stove on real quick, and they'll go right in it.

T: Right into the fire and get all burned.

C: (*Picks up a toy table.*) Who broke this?

T: Who could have done that?

C: Well, I don't like it. Everything is getting broken, and I won't fix it. Whoever broke it, they'll fix it. (*Picks up pieces of doll furniture and places them in different rooms of the dollhouse.*) We'll have two bedrooms and two basements. And the bathroom goes right in there, doesn't it?

T: Wherever you want to put it.

C: And here's the kitchen, and the toilet.

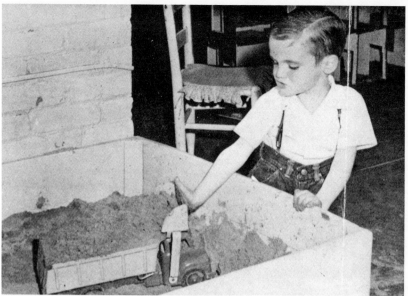

ANGER AS AN EXPRESSION OF FEAR
Robert pushes the dump truck with anger. His real desire is to mess in the sand, but he is afraid at this point in play therapy, as he kneels outside the sand box.

DIFFUSE DISPLAY OF ANGER
Richard strikes out everywhere in anger. He splatters paints all over the easel and floor, smears and pokes his painting, and mixes paints in the water pail. Richard releases pent-up hostility, but without definite focus or direction.

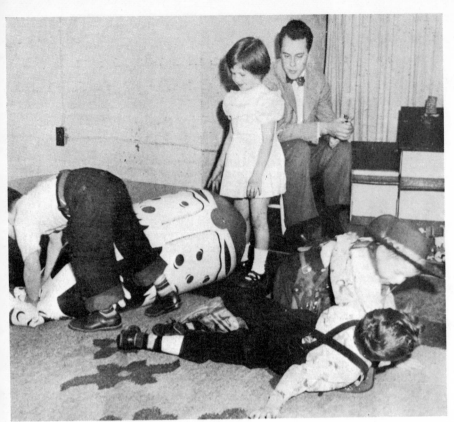

Permission of the Merrill-Palmer School and Miss Donna Harris, Photographer.

GROUP CONFLICT
Nicky attacks the clown while Diane, uncertain of her feelings, looks on. Dave and Cammie fight for the right to furnish the house. The therapist accepts their behavior (as long as no one is hurt) and permits the children to work out their own solutions.

Permission of the Merrill-Palmer School and Miss Donna Harris, Photographer.

LOVE FOR FAMILY
Roy makes "these big cupcakes for all my family," conveying his positive feelings.

REGRESSION: IMMATURITY IN PLAY
Mary pours the water from the nursing bottle into the finger paints and,
giggling, says, "I want it all water to
mess it on the paper."

WISH FOR FREEDOM
Money means everything. Mary explains her unrealistic attitude as follows: "I am going to get all the money
in the world. Then I can be what I
want."

HOSTILITY TOWARD THE BABY
Diane watches intently as the water spills out, and plays through her feelings of aggression toward the new baby.

DELIGHT IN THE BABY'S CRY
Diane says, "I am squeezing her eyes to make her cry. I like to hear her cry." Later Diane shows she also loves the baby, kissing her and dancing around the room.

T: Mm-hm.

C: And this is the room when company comes. Company could go to this company house, couldn't they?

T: Mm-hm.

C: And this is for play. This is the playroom.

T: So they have a playroom, too.

C: Yes. And up here they can put the sick people. (*Suddenly stops. Picks up a knife.*) I'll cut you—cut you to pieces.

T: You want to cut me, hm?

C: Yes. I'll cut you if you talk to me.

T: You don't want me to say anything else, or you'll cut me.

C: Yes. I'll cut you. Cut you wide open. (*Stares at therapist a long time, then drops the knife. Continues to furnish house.*) Here's a table.

T: Mm-hm.

C: You said something! I'll shoot you.

T: You not only feel like shooting me, but you are going to shoot me.

C: Yes. Because I want to.

T: You want to shoot me, hm?

C: Yes. You said something, so I'll shoot you.

T: If I talk, you'll shoot.

C: Yes.

T: You're sure about that.

C: Yes. You said something! I'm going to shoot you, and I'll cut you up.

T: You'll cut me right up, hm?

C: Yeah.

T: That's what you feel like doing.

C: Yeah. (*Puts a few more pieces of doll furniture into the house, leaving considerable space in each room. Then walks away from the house and moves to the vise.*) I'm gonna take this apart. (*Laughs as she takes vise apart.*) Goody, goody.

T: There, you took it apart, and you're glad.

C: Yes. (*Points to Mickey Mouse tractor.*) What can he do? Why does he ride something? (*Turns the head around a few times.*) I'll teach him.

T: You really fixed him.

C: (*Picks up a gun.*) How does this shoot?

T: It's hard to do, isn't it?

C: Yes. Make it shoot.

T: In here you have to do things for yourself, Linda.

C: (*Goes to the dollhouse and starts shooting at it.*)

T: Bang.

C: (*Shoots gun four more times.*)

T: You shot four times.

C: No, I'll shoot eleven times. (*Continues to shoot gun.*)

T: Eleven times.

C: Yes. Because I wanted to. (*Drops gun and continues to furnish dollhouse. Then goes to clay and starts pounding it with her fists.*) I'll paint this clay.

T: You're going to paint it, hm?

C: Yes.

T: You only have a short while longer left today, Linda. Then we'll have to stop.

C: (*Shouts loudly and angrily.*) Why?

T: Because thats all the time you have.

C: I won't go! I don't want to go back there. Not ever.

T: You don't want to go back, hm? But that's all the time we have.

C: Why? Why? Why? Why? Why? (*Pause.*) Here. Open these. (*Hands therapist paint jars.*)

T: Pretty hard to do, aren't they?

C: (*Returns paint jars to workbench and picks up a balloon.*) What's this doing down here?

T: It's just there for whatever you want to use it.

C: (*Picks up jar of blue paint and pushes up her sleeves.*) I'm gonna paint with my hands. I'm gonna paint the whole floor. (*Pulls out paints and paints the floor. Opens red and yellow paint jars and uses these colors for the floor. Then takes a piece of paper and makes patterns on it with finger paints.*) I'm gonna take this back to school with me, because I did it, and I want it. (*Pause.*) I wish you'd move all these things out and have them in nursery school over there.

T: You'd like to have them all over there, hm?

C: (*Rubs paints all over her hands.*) There. Cake. Cake.

T: Making a cake, hm?

C: Yes. Put clay in it and get it all over my hands. I'll paint the clay. I want to take this picture home.

T: When it dries I'll bring it to nursery school, and then you can take it home.

C: I want to take it home now.

T: It's too wet to take now. Well, Linda, your time is up. We'll have to stop for today.

C: No! I won't come!

T: You have to come now.

C: When—when I—when I come, you have to stay here all by yourself. You have to stay here for a lotta weeks. You never can go and eat or anything.

T: You want me to just stay here all the time, is that it?

C: Yes. I'm gonna wash my hands. I'll wash them right on the floor here. (*Rinses hands in water on floor and starts to splash the therapist.*)

T: No, Linda, you may not splash me with the water.

C: Why?·

T: Because I cannot let you do it.

C: Well, I'm going out here to wash my hands.

Discussion: Sixth Play Session

Linda's first actions are expressions of resentment and perhaps hatred. She focuses her attitudes and negative feelings on the therapist, wanting to throw water on the rug and stamp water in his face. She tricks him into opening the vise and laughs in his face, showing the intensity of her feelings and indicating her resentment with "You found out."

When Linda is told she cannot be permitted to throw water in the therapist's face, she does not withdraw and become dependent and passive as she has in the past. Instead she expresses her angry feelings in another way, throwing water all over the playroom floor and stamping around in it.

Linda shows hostile feelings against people in general, asking that the playroom door be locked and threatening to splash anyone who enters.

Later in the session Linda's behavior changes, and she expresses positive feelings for the first time. She furnishes the dollhouse, using all the rooms and leaving space for company. This is in contrast to her earlier behavior of cramming every piece of doll furniture in one small room of the house.

Linda's hostility toward the therapist returns. She shouts at him, threatens to cut him wide open and shoot him if he talks.

From this point to the end of the session Linda fluctuates between shooting at the dollhouse (which possibly represents her family situation) and attempting to create a nice comfortable home atmosphere. This behavior shows mixed feelings, positive and negative, toward her family and home situation, whereas earlier her expression had been entirely negative.

Realizing she has but a short time left to play, Linda becomes upset again and generally hostile. She paints the playroom floor and shouts at the therapist. The negative feelings are shorter in duration and more moderate in intensity than before. Linda proceeds to make a finger painting, working spontaneously and freely. Toward the end of the session she shows self-regard, as she refers to her painting and says, "I'm gonna take this back to school with me, because I did it, and I want it."

Eighth Play Session with Linda

Linda continued to express hostility against people in her play by her violent and unrestrained attacks on the comeback clown during the first twenty minutes of this session. During the last half of the session her behavior fluctuated. First she calmly built a house. Later she destroyed it, called it a "dummy-bum house," and scattered it throughout the room. At the end of the session she painted joyfully and seemed proud of what she had made.

C: (*Walks into the room and goes to the doll figures. Laughs.*) How many dolls here? Seven. (*Laughs again.*) Look. I broke one. (*Removes the head of the mother figure.*)

T: Mm-hm. You broke one, and you don't care.

C: (*Takes all the clothes off the doll figures.*) I'm gonna throw all the clothes in the water. (*Throws clothes into pail of water. Then picks up a dressing table and places it in the dollhouse. Opens roof of house.*) Look. They can walk into that room and that room and through here. They have fun.

And they can look out the window. They can go up and
down. (*Pause.*) I'm not gonna furnish their house up.

T: You're not going to furnish it, hm?

C: Nope. Not for anyone! Just throw it in there. (*Throws the dolls
into the dollhouse.*)

T: Throw them right in, hm?

C: Yes. Everything. And I don't care.

T: You don't care what happens.

C: Yes. I don't care if anyone gets broke. I'll just throw them in
there anyway.

T: You don't care about that. You'll just throw them in anyway.

C: (*Picks up a toilet and places it in dollhouse.*) They can walk
into the bathroom and out through there. (*Stares at dollhouse for a while.*) Look. It's funny. A funny house.

T: Mm-hm.

C: I'm making it that way because it is that way.

T: You're making it funny because that's the way you feel about it.

C: Yes. (*Pause. Points to the comeback toy.*) Look at him. He's a
clown with two faces and two heads.

T: He's an old smarty.

C: Yes, he is. (*Picks up a balloon and squeezes it.*) I'm gonna bust
this balloon into pieces.

T: You'll rip it apart, hm?

C: Yeah. And make them all bust.

T: You'll make them all bust.

C: Yes. (*Throws balloons into pail of water. Runs to comeback
and hits it in the face.*) I smacked him. Gave him a good
smack.

T: You got him right in the face.

C: Goody!

T: You're glad about it, hm?

C: Now I'll finish him up. I'll throw water on it. I'll drip it all over
him.

T: You're really going to get him all over.

C: Yeah. (*Hits comeback several times, first in the stomach, then
in the face. Pulls comeback around the room.*) I'm going to
make him go all the way down to the floor. I'll punch him
right in the face.

T: You'll really bust him.

C: And I'll make his eyes go away.

T: And then he won't be able to see.

C: No, he won't. But I will.

T: Mm-hm. And you will. Just you and me will be able to see then, hm?

C: (*Splashes water all over comeback and shouts.*) You big old dumb-bum! (*Pulls comeback toward pail.*) Now I'll stick his head down in the water.

T: You'll smack him right down there.

C: He's a dummy. He's a dummy. I'm gonna throw the water all over the whole place.

T: You want to just throw it everywhere.

C: (*Fills toy bathtub and throws water around the room.*) Now there, that takes care of it. Now I'll throw it on the clown.

T: You want to throw it at the clown.

C: Look what a mess. There, I gave it to him. (*Pushes comeback down to floor and jumps back with a frightened look as comeback starts to rise.*) He can't get up, can he? He can't get up.

T: Are you afraid that he might?

C: (*Laughs. Splashes more water on the comeback.*) He got it again. Right on his head.

T: Right on his head.

C: Another head.

T: Mm-hm.

C: I'm gonna pour the whole thing on him.

T: Mm-hm.

C: Help me. Help me pour it on him.

T: You want me to help you, but in here you have to do things for yourself.

C: I'm gonna step on him if he don't lay down.

T: He'll either lay down or you'll step on him.

C: Yes. Now I'll make him dirtier and dirtier. (*Breathes heavily as she pushes comeback and hits it. Watches it come up slowly and then pushes it down again. Tries to keep comeback down by putting part of it under a table.*) Stay down!

You stay down! You keep him down. I'll put the chair beside him. There.

T: He's lying down now.

C: (*Picks up pail of water and throws water on comeback. Walks around, stamping in water, and chants.*) Dumb-dumb-dumb. Dumb-dumb-dumb-dumb. Dumb-dumb-dumb-dumb. Dumb-dumb-dumb. (*Throws remaining drops of water in pail on comeback.*) I'm going out and get some more. (*Fills pail with more water from bathroom.*) He's gonna get splashed again.

T: Yes. You'll give it to him again.

C: I'm gonna throw it on his eye first.

T: You really splattered him.

C: I splattered him all over. (*Drops pail and walks to box of blocks.*) Now I'm gonna build him a house. And my house is gonna be bigger than ever. Why do you have the blocks?

T: You wonder about that.

C: For no one to play.

T: They're not for anybody, hm?

C: No. Just me.

T: Only you. No one else. No one but you.

C: No. No one but me.

T: Mm-hm.

C: (*Finishes building a house of blocks.*) There. This house is a dummy-bum.

T: A dummy-bum house.

C: Yes. Because they're dumb.

T: Mm-hm.

C: (*Picks up blocks and throws them against the wall. Laughs very loudly.*) I almost hit that.

T: Yes, you almost hit the mirror, but I cannot let you throw blocks at that.

C: (*Starts to throw blocks into pail of water.*) I'll throw them in the water. Look. I hit it. Hit the pail.

T: Mm-hm.

C: I'm gonna take all the blocks and throw them right in there. (*Picks up the masks. Tries them on and laughs as she puts each one on.*) Now I'm gonna play with this piece of clay. (*Pounds clay on table.*)

T: Linda, you have only a short while longer to play.

C: (*Puts some red paint on the paper. Then covers whole sheet with red, yellow, and blue paint.*) Look. Look what I made.

T: Mm-hm.

C: Is my time up for today?

T: You only have a couple of minutes left.

C: Why?

T: That's all the time left.

C: Because I have to go back to school. (*Makes another painting, using all three colors.*) See? I'm making this here.

T: Mm-hm.

C: There. It's finished. Can you bring my pictures when they're dry?

T: You like what you've made?

C: Yes. You put them up to dry and bring them to me later.

T: All right, I'll do that. Your time is up for now.

Discussion: Eighth Play Session

Linda begins by expressing anger and resentment, possibly toward her mother, removing the head of the mother-doll figure and laughing loudly. There are, however, more positive feelings in her play in this session as compared to previous sessions. She shows ambivalence toward the family. Using family figures, she throws all their clothes in water. Then, positively, she lets the family dolls explore the "spacious" house and indicates the numerous conveniences they have. Linda becomes resentful again and exclaims, "I'm not gonna furnish their house." She throws the family dolls into the house and does not care what happens to them. Linda wants to "bust the balloons into pieces," hits the humanlike comeback toy in the stomach and face a number of times, and expresses a desire to blind him. The comeback may represent her father, who has been critical of Linda and has called her "dumb" frequently. Apparently Linda retaliates with "You big old dumb-bum!" She repeats this phrase again and again and then, sticks "his head down in the water." When the therapist wonders if

Linda is afraid he will strike back, Linda laughs and splashes more water on the comeback and holds his head under the water, shouting, "dumb, dumb, dumb."

Later in the session Linda's feelings toward "him" are more positive. She says, "Now I'm gonna build *him* a house. And his house is gonna be bigger than ever." However, she becomes ambivalent again and is uncertain whether the house is a good house or a "dummy-bum" house. Linda spends the remaining time painting and proudly asks to take her paintings home.

Linda's experiences in play therapy may be summarized as follows: Her initial attitudes were characterized largely by negative feelings and intense anxiety. As her anxiety lessened, a form of generalized anger appeared. At first the anger was directed toward the therapist but later toward the mother and father. As more and more of the negative feelings were expressed and explored in the therapeutic relationship, positive feelings began to emerge. At the end of the eighth session Linda felt worthwhile as a person, accepted herself, and liked what she did. She also showed more acceptance of her parents. Unfortunately, Linda had not fully worked through her hostile and ambivalent attitudes toward her family and would have possibly benefited from additional play therapy experiences.

The nursery school staff reported considerable change in Linda's behavior in school, and the mother indicated that a number of changes had occurred at home. After her third play session, the school notified the therapist that Linda was beginning to play with other children. For the first time in her two years at nursery school, she told a story to the children and led a group of children in a number of rhythms. She no longer spoke in a whining tone, and she was more decisive and free in her play. Her teacher said that Linda was participating in discussion periods. She was surprised, too, that Linda was participating in the rhythms, when at one time she could not be induced to take part in them. Her teacher reported also that now Linda had two friends in school with whom she played frequently.

In conferences with Linda's teacher, sometime after her eighth session, it was reported that the above changes had become even broader, and that Linda was much happier in school. Her teacher stated that the most outstanding difference seemed to be that Linda was expressing her feelings clearly.

Reported changes in the nursery school were supplemented by the mother's comments in her counseling contacts. The mother described Linda as a much less frightened child, more sociable, and more considerate of others in the family.

CAROL

Carol, an only child, four years old, was referred to the play therapist by a community agency. Mrs. L, Carol's mother, was considerably worried about Carol's recent complaints of stomach pains during mealtimes. Also, Carol's habit of twisting and pulling her hair had become so serious that she was partially bald.

Family background data included the following: the mother's repeated statement that Carol looked and acted like a stepsister whom the mother hated; the mother's strong emphasis on cleanliness, and the degradation she felt in her own family experiences, where her stepparents were alcoholics and her home was usually littered with scraps of food and dirt; the parents' belief that Carol was incapable of loving them or anyone; and the crowded conditions in the family's seven-room house, where they lived with three other families.

Mrs. L was seen regularly by a caseworker. The play therapist had two interviews with Carol's mother. The first of these was held before Carol's first play session. After the final play session a second interview was conducted. Attitudes expressed in the last interview will be described later. A summary of Mrs. L's attitudes toward Carol, as expressed in the first recorded interview, follows.

"I can't accomplish anything with her. She just won't listen. You have to use force. You just can't treat her nice and expect to get results. . . . I punish her frequently, and then she becomes a very, very good girl, but it makes me feel like a worm afterwards. But then, at her age, she just can't understand anything but that kind of treatment. . . . She's just very selfish, and that's all there is to it. What makes me so mad is that she's so quick to notice when someone else is selfish, but she herself continues to be a selfish person. . . . She just seems to be getting worse and worse. . . . She's pulling her hair out all the time, and she always complains about her stomach at meals."

Carol's mother saw her as a selfish, inconsiderate, disagreeable, unruly child with stomach pains and hair-twisting symptoms. The therapist found her to be a frightened, lonely, love-hungry, confused, and hostile child. Carol had twenty-one play therapy contacts. During this time she expressed her attitudes of resentment, hatred, loneliness, and fear. She explored these feelings and attitudes, expressed them again and again, and reexplored them.

Tremendous feelings against the mother were prominent in these sessions. Carol struggled to free herself of these torturing emotions and eventually gained a degree of emotional and intellectual insight within herself. This meant that Carol could see herself more clearly as a person and understand how her relations with others might improve through a sincere desire to share and cooperate. During the first few contacts Carol often spoke in a language of her own that was not understandable. Later she expressed herself clearly and intelligently. After the fourth play session the mother reported that Carol's stomach pains had disappeared. Carol expressed more respect for herself and a greater affection toward others. As a way of illustrating Carol's growth, excerpts from the recorded play sessions follow.

First Play Session with Carol

(*Mother enters the room with Carol.*)
M: Isn't this lovely?
C: Mm-hm.
M: Do you like this?
C: Mm-hm.
M: Now you play down here. O.K.?
C: Mm-hm.
M: Then I'll go see Mrs. D. O.K.?
C: Mm-hm.
M: All right.
C: Mm-hm.
M: And I'll come back and get you. O.K.?
C: Mm-hm.
M: He's going to watch you, darling. O.K.?

C: Mm-hm.

M: O.K.?

C: Mm-hm.

M: O.K.?

C: Mm-hm.

M: Do you want to kiss Mommy? (*Kisses Carol's cheek.*) O.K.?

C: Mm-hm.

M: I'll be back. O.K.?

C: Mm-hm.

M: All right. Bye-bye.

C: Bye.

M: (*Walks out of the room after looking back at Carol.*)

Throughout the session Carol constantly refers to worn toys and at the end says, "I guess the kids don't break 'em. I guess the people who bring 'em in just break 'em first and then let the kids play with 'em."

Second Play Session with Carol

C: I'm gonna use this stick to paint with.

T: You are?

C: Mm-hm. I'm not messing up my hands. I'm gonna use all of these.

T: All the colors, hm?

C: That's what I'm gonna do. Use all of them. That's what I always do. (*Pause.*) We have much troubles. Much troubles.

T: You really have trouble, don't you?

C: Mm-hm. I'm gonna wash my hands.

T: You don't like to have your hands dirty.

C: I don't much. No, I won't wash my hands now. I'll wait before I go upstairs.

T: You're going to wash them before you go upstairs, hm?

C: I don't want my mommy to see them dirty.

T: You don't want her to know about it.

. . . . . .

C: (*Picks up nursing bottle and chews on the nipple. Drinks for a while and then starts chewing again.*) Looks like I'll have to stay here nineteen years.

T: A long, long time, isn't it?

C: Just for this old bottle.

T: That will keep you here if nothing else does.

C: Yes. (*Laughs and continues to drink. Chews nipple for quite a while.*)

T: Just keep working and working and working on it, hm?

C: My mommy is going to have to wait until I get to be four years old.

T: She'll have to wait until you grow up to be four, hm?

C: Yes. (*Sighs heavily and continues to chew nipple.*)

. . . . . .

C: I'm gonna shoot up this whole place.

T: Just shoot everything, hm?

C: Yeah. (*Laughs shrilly.*)

T: Shooting all over.

C: (*Laughs.*) I'm shooting everybody in the place.

T: Everybody is being shot down, hm?

C: Everybody except my girl friend.

T: She's the only one you won't shoot.

C: Yeah. I'm gonna shoot you now. (*Laughs.*) Why don't you fall down?

T: You'd like me to just fall.

C: Uh-huh. After I shoot you, you can stay up just one minute. Then you be dead. (*Shoots at therapist and laughs.*) You don't get up.

T: Not ever to get up.

C: You never get up. Nobody's gonna see. I'm gonna shoot the lights off.

Discussion: Play Sessions One and Two

The mother seems considerably anxious in leaving Carol, asking repeatedly for permission to leave. Left with the therapist, Carol chatters incessantly, points to the toys but does not play with them, and in other ways shows diffuse anxiety. At the end of the first session she expresses hostile feelings toward adults, rather tentatively but directly, saying that people who bring children to the playroom (in Carol's case, her mother) break the toys first and "then let the kids play with 'em."

Carol conveys the attitude that her home is filled with troubles and shows fear of her mother. She becomes immature in her play, drinks from the nursing bottle and chews the nipple. She shows hostility toward her mother and implies that her mother is responsible for her immaturity, saying, "My mommy is going to have to wait until I get to be four years old."

Carol's negative expressions become more generalized. In her play she shoots all the humanlike figures in the room, except one doll which she identifies as her girl friend. She is especially vehement against the therapist, shooting him and telling him to die and never get up. At the end of the second session she shoots off all the lights, so that no one will see the "crimes" she has committed in her fantasy.

Fourth Play Session with Carol

C: (*Designates an area while playing in the sand.*) That stuff you see is halfway up to the north.

T: Halfway up to the north, hm?

C: Yes. And this north has a monster. The other north has nothing in it except trees.

T: Nothing but trees.

C: The other north is wild.

T: Two norths. A wild one and a peaceful one.

C: You can get lost in it. You could get lost all over till you go straight. Then you could get to the cars. You get to the cars, and then you walk a little further, and then you get to my farm. You got a driveway going up there. 'Way up on the hill.

T: Mm-hm.

C: Yes. Mine's 'way up there on the hill.

T: Your farm's up high?

C: No. I changed it to a house.

T: Just changed your mind.

C: Ain't it looking perfect now? This is where the seeds grow. And they're gonna grow up, and stuff is gonna be all around here. Don't you see? Don't you see the house here?

T: Mm-hm.

C: And there's going to be stairs going up here.

T: I see.

C: And this is going to be a room right through part of the house. This was the rough place, but you can pat it right down like this. It's a house. It's a house. Don't you know?

T: It's a house.

C: It's a house. Not a real toy.

T: It's a real house.

C: Yeah. The whole thing is big. It's all one house.

T: Mm-hm.

C: And this house is gonna storm now.

T: Really going to storm.

C: Many years ago it stormed down.

T: It was all broken down then.

C: Yes. You see, this part's gonna come off.

T: Tear right down.

C: Just this part. Just the roof.

T: Mm-hm.

C: And there's a safety zone down here to save the people. The people come down to here after the storm. Then they come back here and build it up again. Then the storm comes again and blows it away. Then the people come and put it up again.

T: Mm-hm.

C: This part here is gonna be a secret panel so the people will never know what a big house.

T: They'll never know the truth about it.

C: That's right. At night is when the storm comes up, and then comes the morning, and then they can build it up safely so that it won't come down again.

T: Mm-hm.

C: It all looks different now.

T: Not the same any more.

C: Don't you know what happened in the storm? It all fell. This is gonna be a special one. She didn't like the other one, and she never will.

T: She never liked it.

C: It'll be all zoomed up here. You wouldn't like *your* house to fall. Well, the storm—. She must have got the bad lady. Her didn't like anybody except the house cooker.

T: She liked only the house cooker.

C: Mm-hm. Who cleaned her house. She didn't like the strange people. They got her then. They got her right down, and that was the end of her. No. That wasn't. That was the end of the people.

T: All of them died?

C: Except the good ones. It all happened years and years ago.

T: Many, many years ago.

C: That's when I was a baby. And the storms came and tore everything apart. Now the whole thing's crashed down. (*Stands back and surveys sand pile.*) I'm all done with that. That finishes that job. (*Picks up clay and flattens two small pieces of clay.*) Everything's always the same.

T: Nothing ever changes here.

C: I have to shine my glasses. *Some* glasses she gave me. I'm gonna tell her this is no good. It's not even glass.

T: She gave you some pretty poor glasses, hm?

C: I'll take 'em back. They're not even glasses. There. Now listen, I want some good glasses back. (*Pretends to open a package.*) Same old glasses!

T: She's given you the rotten ones again.

C: I'll take them back and see what she'll give me this time. Oh, lookit. Oh, oh, how pretty shined they *look.* But they're still the *same* old thing.

T: You've been cheated so many times, haven't you?

C: I'll take them back. Now let me try these. They look shiny. But they're no good.

T: Every time they look so good, and they turn out to be so bad.

C: Well, *this* time she gets some good ones. Now what is she going to have for lunch? (*Continues to play with the clay.*) Half a motorcycle and a little butter. I guess I'll wrap it up. She told me that I'd like it. If you don't eat it, you're gonna get a licking. Let's see if this would be butter. Oh, it should be. It's good work stuff. Aah, gee, that's supposed to be butter? That's butter I'm getting? Oh, I hate it, I hate it.

Turn it over. Mix it up. Are you gonna eat it? I wouldn't. What's it supposed to be? Now he'll find out what he's getting. But he won't like it. She sure don't fix his lunch. She fixes it the rotten way. He's gonna fix his own, and he won't fix another rotten one. This man sure is a good kind. Good as gooder. (*Pause.*) Oh, this tastes so good. Now I'm gonna kill some of this clay if she don't know any better. She sure gave me some rotten stuff. I'll see what she says about this piece. If you couldn't eat it, then you can't. Let's see what she says about this stuff that she wanted. If she do that again, she'll get some bad. Oh, what she does! One slice she gives. One slice and one slice and one slice. Oh, I hope you got the good food you wanted. Do you want good food? You're getting it. Here, I'm giving it away. She won't like it but she gives mine away, and I don't like that. It's a good thing you're sitting over there, because I don't want to get any cutting on you. (*Looks at therapist.*) You might get cut open.

T: I might just get cut open if I weren't over here.

C: Mm-hm. Might get cut and ruined. Do you mind if I wrap it up and throw it away? I don't want it any more.

T: That's up to you.

C: She'll find out it was me.

T: And are you afraid?

C: She gave me dumb. Well, she's gonna have dumb right back.

T: You'll give it to her right back, hm?

C: If she gives it to me again, she's gonna get it right back.

T: You mean you'll give it to her if she does it again?

C: She will. You should hear her when she starts. She started it years and years back.

T: It all started a long time ago.

C: Yes. Now see what she says about this stuff. She's not gonna like it.

T: You won't let her get away with it, hm?

C: She won't never get away with it with me. I'll tie her up and say that I'm moving.

T: If you have to, that's what you'll do.

C: I'll move even if I don't have to. I'll move anyway. (*Picks up small nursing bottle and sprinkles clay.*) Squirt, squirt. I'm gonna squirt her. See how she gets it now.

T: She's getting it now, hm?

C: She will get it. She won't like it the way I'm gonna fix it. She'll get it the same old way.

T: You'll give it to her just like she gave it to you, hm?

C: Because I don't like hers. I won't eat her food. I'll eat the other people's food. Their food is better.

T: Her food makes you feel bad.

C: I'm gonna cut her open and see her. Here's your old sicky food.

T: You'll cut her right open and give it back to her.

C: She'll say, "Ah, what kind of food is this?" And she'll say, "That's good; it must be good." But it won't be.

T: If she says it's good, it probably won't be.

C: Probably I'll put poison in it. I'll put it in it.

T: Poison in the food.

C: Yeah. And if she says it's good, she'll find out.

T: She'll find out if she eats it.

C: How you like this food? It won't make you die. This will be much gooder. Some of this is so good. And some of it's got poison in it.

T: Some is good and some is bad, hm?

C: She'll say it's all good when it isn't. And she'll eat it. Aah! I'm dying. Thought it was good food. Some good food you called it. Rascal food. Now I'll put some good food in it. Some real good stuff. I'm gonna cut her open and get all that bad food out. And put some good food in. It's good food, but she thinks it's poison. She thinks she's dying. She's just making herself dead.

T: She thinks she's dying and making herself dead.

C: Mm-hm. She won't be. She'll be alive as anything. This is good food. I'm getting hungry as could be, so I better eat this good food that I got her. Wow! I'm afraid! I hope I don't die.

T: You're afraid to eat the food, is that it?

C: No, thank you. Now I've got a good bite to eat. So I guess I'll go on to the good part. (*Runs back to play in the sand.*)

Discussion: Fourth Play Session

Carol expresses a number of mixed emotions in this session. She creates two norths, a peaceful one and a wild one, which in her own mind may represent her ambivalent feelings toward her own home situation. She makes a house in the sand, destroys it, builds it again, destroys it, reenacting this play sequence a number of times.

Carol's despair and loneliness seem very great as she looks at the therapist and says, "You wouldn't like *your* house to fall." She conveys the emptiness of her emotional life and attributes it to the fact that "she must have got the bad lady," who didn't like anybody and was interested only in cooking and cleaning. Carol indicates it all happened when she was a baby, "and the storms came and tore everything apart."

Carol's anger becomes direct and she shows, possibly, how her mother has always deceived her and cheated her. Her feelings are severe in intensity, and her sarcasm mounts. She reveals hatred for her mother, who has always tricked her and withheld her love. In the play situation Carol retaliates, expresses hostility toward her mother, and poisons her. Later in the session Carol shows the positive side of her feelings toward her mother in her desire to be loved. She takes "all that bad food out" and gives the mother good food.

Fifth Play Session with Carol

C: (*Kneels in sandbox and builds with the sand.*) Four years ago a rock—a rock felled on this house. So we call it a part of the house.

T: Four years ago a rock fell in it?

· · · · · ·

C: (*Plays in the sandbox.*) She turns it up herself, and she plays all around and has a lot of fun. That's the way it should be. She used to laugh, but not Mama.

T: She laughed, but her mama didn't, hm?

C: Her mama used to holler all she could. She'd holler and holler and holler. All she wanted was a house. Not a big house. Just a little girl's size.

· · · · · ·

C: (*Plays in the sandbox.*) Now she says now it looks like a house. She screams out, and ever since she's crying. It's different, this house. First the daddy left the mother, and now the mother left the daddy.

T: Mm-hm. Daddy left Mommy and Mommy left Daddy.

C: So you know what she did? She built herself a house her size. She crashed down the house to make her own house.

T: She made a house all of her own.

C: Nobody lived in it except her, and everybody's happy now. Except her. So she's cut her's off again.

T: She didn't want her house attached to theirs.

C: So she moved it down to California, and they didn't like it. But she loved it. And they didn't like it.

T: So she moved away.

C: And she brought water for her house. A little water. Water in a tub for her house. All around the house, water, water, water. And her house is bigger. And her house is bigger and bigger and bigger. Finally she wanted it hooked on again. So you know what she did? She moved again and hooked hers on. So they were glad. And their family wasn't happy, and she was happy. Before, they were happy and she wasn't happy. So what's the difference?

T: She's happy now, and they aren't.

C: So she crashed her house down again and made another one. If they wanted to hook on, she didn't mind.

T: She would let them hook on, hm?

C: Only how could they hook on, the way they had built it?

Sixth Play Session with Carol

C: (*Builds large mounds in the sand.*) I want to be warm.

T: You want to be warm.

C: It's rock cold.

T: Cold as rock.

C: Colder than rock.

T: Mm-hm. Quite cold.

C: You'll never know.

Seventh Play Session with Carol

C: (*Sits in front of the dollhouse and plays with doll figures.*) My hands are ice cold. What kind of water is this? It's so cold. Turn on some hot water. No. We don't have any hot water. But there *was* hot water. It *was* hot water. It's just so cold. If you do what I say, you can get out of there and have hot water. *Now* do you understand? So they had to do what she said.

T: They have to do what she says in order to get warm water.

C: They can't do what she says. We're stuck in with glue. Too bad we can't. Be quiet, they shout. So they did be quiet. They can't hear my noise, but they can hear their noise. See what they did? They told you to get out of the house. Now get out! And I mean get out! (*Pause.*) Finally. But—hey, hey, it's cold out. It's cold out anyway. Be quiet yourselves. This house is not for big people like you. So they took a gun and shot them one by one.

. . . . . .

C: (*Still playing with doll figures.*) They're so cold here. Even the horses had to go outside. It's lucky they had a heater. But she got colder and colder. She just couldn't stand it. She just couldn't stand it.

. . . . . .

C: (*Handles clay at workbench.*) I guess I'll put on these aprons. Aprons, aprons, aprons. Guess I'll put on two aprons, because I'm gonna get awful dirty. (*Picks up scissors and jabs at clay.*) Zhoop, zhoop, zhoop, zhoop, zhoop, zhoop. Oh, goody! She's stabbed. She used to think about this stuff that was good. She used to dream about it. So Mommy could fix it up so she liked it. How did she dream about it? How did she used to do it? She used to say, "Give me the porcher, porcher, porcher. Give me the porcher, porcher." Boy! Was that ever good!

EIGHTH PLAY SESSION WITH CAROL

C: (*Plays with doll figures while sitting in front of the dollhouse.*)
    She calls them good, only they're bad. Because Mom calls
    them good, she calls them bad. Mom calls them good, but
    she calls them bad. They don't agree on that. (*Pause.*)
    Here's another one that she likes. But Mom says this one's
    bad too. And she likes the bad ones.

T: She likes the bad ones, does she?

C: Mm-hm.

NINTH PLAY SESSION WITH CAROL

C: (*Plays with the clay and the vise.*) I'm gonna smash it in two.
    Wanta see me smash it?

T: You're going to smash it in two, hm?

C: (*Pushes the clay into the vise.*)

T: Carol, you have only a short while longer to play. Just a few
    minutes more.

C: A few minutes? I don't care about that.

T: Just a few minutes.

C: It's long enough. Isn't the Fourth of July long enough? It's
    long enough. I have to grind this up now. (*Puts more clay
    into vise and handles it for a few minutes.*) I'm through.
    Can't stay here all day. Next time I come, I'm gonna do it
    backwards. Start with the clay, then the dollhouse and the
    sandbox.

T: You know exactly what you're going to do.

C: And after that I'm gonna start with these balloons.

T: You've got it all planned out.

C: Yeah. I started it all.

T: And now you're going to finish it.

C: Mm-hm. It's all in pieces now.

Discussion: Play Sessions Five through Nine

Carol shows how lonely and cold her life has been; in her play
"she used to laugh," but "her mama used to holler." She seems to
indicate strained relations between her parents, their rejection of
each other and of her. Carol makes a house in the sand "all her

own" but is dissatisfied and unhappy with it. She is uncertain. She wants to be near her parents and love them. Yet she is afraid. In her play she fluctuates between moving away from them and staying near them, exclaiming, "If they wanted to hook on [to her house], she didn't mind." In earlier play sessions Carol was determined to move away permanently.

Carol repeatedly expresses her feelings of loneliness. "My hands are ice cold," she screams, and later, "But she got colder and colder. She just couldn't stand it. She just couldn't stand it."

She expresses hostility toward adults again in her play, shooting all the adult doll figures one by one.

She regresses in her play and speaks immaturely.

Carol plays out her conflicts with her mother numerous times and shows how strongly they disagree. As the ninth session ends she shows growth in her ability to decide and play, saying, "Next time I come, I'm gonna do it backwards. Start with the clay, then the dollhouse and the sandbox. And after that I'm gonna start with these balloons."

TENTH PLAY SESSION WITH CAROL

C: (*Plays with the clay and vise.*) You put this in here. This is the last time I'm getting into this. This is the only time. Then I'll forget about the whole thing.

T: Mm-hm. This is the last of it then.

C: I don't care about cutting. I just cared about the clay.

. . . . . .

C: (*Still playing with clay.*) Squawking all the time. I don't like that.

T: You don't want that, hm?

C: Squawk, squawk. That's all they figure. They just can't help it. Squawk, squawk. That's all they can squawk. Squawk, squawk. That's all they'll get back. If I don't get it, then I won't give it. I get squawk, squawk. Something else. That's what I'd like. Something else.

T: You wish they'd give you something besides squawking.

C: Talk, talk. Squawk, squawk. That's what they do. I'll put a snake in there. See if that squawks. I think the snake does.

Water snake, water snake. You go in there. I'm home, snake, and my mama won't let me go out any more. Squawk, squawk. Squawking all the time.

ELEVENTH PLAY SESSION WITH CAROL

C: All you do is sit, sit, sit. Well, I don't want you to do anything more.

T: You feel that that's enough.

C: Just that and nothing more.

TWELFTH PLAY SESSION WITH CAROL

C: (*Plays with doll figures at the dollhouse.*) Everybody's going to be naked in the family.

T: A whole family without clothes.

C: Then the boys can see the girls, and the girls can see the boys.

T: Each one can see the other.

C: And I can see all the little children with their clothes off. And then they're gonna take *all* the people's clothes off. Not just dollies. All their clothes are gonna come off. The children will see each other.

THIRTEENTH PLAY SESSION WITH CAROL

C: (*Plays with the clay and paper towel.*) I think I'll wrap this up for lunch today.

T: That'll be your lunch, hm?

C: Yes. I guess I'll have this for us to eat. I got it all wrapped up. He *only* has to go to work. To work, to work, to work, to work. She bothers me every day. (*Pause.*) It's so quiet around here today. That's what I want. Just so much peace and quiet.

T: That's what you want most. Just peace and quiet.

C: Because the old mother hollered at me every day. Hollered every day. And all she wants is peace and quiet.

* * * * *

C: No home. No home at all.

T: Not a real home, hm?

C: No house like you have. Like kids have.

T: You don't have a house like other kids, hm?

C: No. In mine it's just the same old things. All I do is walk around and do nothing. That's all I can do.

T: Just walking around with nothing to do.

C: I'll stop now. I'm going upstairs.

FOURTEENTH PLAY SESSION WITH CAROL

C: (*Plays with clay at workbench.*) Look. What a silly. What I'm doing! I'm cutting.

T: You're cutting and being silly.

C: No. I'm not silly. Now, I'm having good things to eat. And I'm selfish. I don't want anyone else to eat my things. (*Pause.*) Do you want something to eat?

T: Do you suppose that I would?

C: Yes. You might like this to eat at home.

FIFTEENTH PLAY SESSION WITH CAROL

C: (*Plays with the clay.*) You know, I live alone.

T: All by yourself, hm?

C: But I have two sisters who live down the street. We fight once in a while, but we get along most of the time. (*Pauses as she fingers clay.*) I don't like boys. They're nasty.

T: You don't like boys.

C: Well, really *they* don't like me. Maybe I'd better go back to work. I'm gonna have lunch. Would you like to eat with me?

Discussion: Play Sessions Ten through Fifteen

Carol again expresses feelings of anger and resentment against her parents. In her play she refers to their constant quarreling and indicates their frequent criticisms of her. She retaliates with "Squawk. Squawk. Squawk. That's all they'll get back."

Later Carol removes the clothing from all the doll figures and implies that if all people were "naked" (perhaps she means without fears and defenses), we could see each other as we really are.

Hostility toward the mother reappears. Carol wishes to escape her mother's persistent admonitions. In a whisper she says, "It's so quiet around here today. That's what I want. Just so much peace and quiet." She indicates the tragedy of her home situation, telling the therapist that she has no home at all, not like other kids.

As the sessions continue, Carol becomes more relaxed and spontaneous in her play. There is even a childishness about her. In previous sessions she has acted more like a miniature adult. She acts silly and laughs continually.

Carol recognizes her selfishness but justifies it, indicating that she has never had good "food," but now "I'm having good things to eat." When her feelings of selfishness are accepted, she offers to share her "food" with the therapist.

Sixteenth Play Session with Carol

C: (*Plays in the sandbox.*) They're gonna have a new house. I think this house is a music house. Ha ha, a music house.

T: That's what. A music house.

C: It's going to be so big that they're gonna have to put some music in this house. They'll have to have a television too. They're gonna crowd the house.

T: They want to crowd the house, hm?

C: But I'll fix it. That piano goes out farther. I'll put it back a little.

T: Mm-hm.

C: All right. A nice little room. How do you like it? Don't it look nicer with the piano spaced out farther?

T: More space there, hm?

C: And in here we'll have a door. It's gonna be a little hideout. And the kids can see their mother at night. And the kids can fool their mother. But the big people—they can just see from the top. And if the mothers go through there to the hideout, then—bang. The whole house gets on fire.

T: That's what would happen, hm? The whole house would catch fire.

C: Now the kids are gonna build themselves another house. And their mothers.

T: Just for the kids and the mothers, hm?

C: No. Just for the kids. And it's gonna be just right.

T: It'll have plenty of room, hm?

C: Yes. Right back here to the house. And they like to play. Right to the back of the house.

T: That certainly will be roomy for them.

C: The kids are gonna have a good time. They'll have pianos. They'll have hundreds of pianos.

T: Hundreds of pianos.

C: Yeah. For a nice big house.

T: They'll enjoy themselves then, with all those pianos.

C: All the kids will be climbing around the pianos and jumping up and down on them and having fun.

EIGHTEENTH PLAY SESSION WITH CAROL

C: (*Plays in the sandbox.*) And then she dreamed another story.

T: She dreamed another story.

C: This is gonna be the whole story she dreamed. She read it in a book once and said, "I'm gonna try and dream it." Then she thought maybe I should get a record of it first and see if it's scary. I don't like anything if it's scary.

T: You don't like scary things, hm?

C: No. I don't like cowboys and shooting. And even animals, if they're big. Every time I hear a noise when I'm up in bed, then I'm scared.

T: When you hear noises while sleeping, you're really afraid, hm?

C: Also when I'm bad sometimes and have to sit in a chair.

T: Oh, when you're bad and hear noises, then you get frightened.

C: Yes. When I hear noises then I'm always scared. My mommy comes and says she doesn't hear it, but I do.

T: You hear it even though your mommy doesn't, and it frightens you.

C: Yes. And it's really only something like the washing machine or somebody pounding.

T: It turns out to be something just silly, but it still frightens you.

C: Yes. It rolls me back.

NINETEENTH PLAY SESSION WITH CAROL

C: (*Plays in the sandbox.*) This isn't a free country. Nobody gets free here. But I made this. I made all my people, but I didn't make them right.

T: You made them, but they didn't turn out the right way.

C: I know things that they don't know. Ha ha ha.

T: You know some things that they don't.

C: This is my girl friend. She likes me, and I like her too. I'm gonna eat my pie with her.

T: You like her, and so you're sharing your pie with her.

C: Yes. We'll eat it. She gets half and I get half. She thinks it's too much for me, but I've been starving to death, so I'll eat it. (*Pause.*) You know, kids just love people, but sometimes people don't love kids.

Twentieth Play Session with Carol

C: (*Plays in the sand and describes the destruction of a village by a huge storm. The people work together to rebuild it.*) If I helped them, then they'd like me, and it will never be crashed again. I'll make a great big cake for them. How deep is my cake gonna be? Oh, my cake, cake, cake. Baking a good, delicious cake. No, I'm gonna eat it all up.

T: Just for you, that cake.

C: Not all of it. I'll divide it up with them, because they're my friends. Friends, friends. *I'm* a friend, and I'm not gonna eat it all. I'm gonna give them some.

. . . . . .

C: (*Plays in the sandbox.*) A lotta times she dreams about castles. She dreams about all this, only it's too late now.

T: Is it too late for her now?

C: Well, maybe not. I'll make one for her. I'm gonna make the castle. I'm gonna make Carol the first castle she's ever had.

T: You're going to do that for her, hm?

C: Yup. And tonight it's gonna be filled all around with pretty water.

. . . . . .

C: See this cake? You can cut it in many pieces. In small pieces for many people.

T: That's the way you want to cut it, hm?

C: The big chiefs get the biggest pieces. Yes, the biggest chiefs always get the biggest pieces.

Final Play Session with Carol

C: (*Plays in the sandbox.*) Nobody knows what I know. Nobody knows what I know. (*Chants.*) Nobody goes where I go.

Nobody wants to go where I go. Nobody wants to go where I go. (*Pause.*) You take the dirt, and you take the water, and you mix it together. Water and sand. Rub it, squeeze it, mix it. That's what you do in here. You mix things the way you want. I'm gonna make *some* pie, I am. And then there won't be any more time. I'm gonna make a pie so big it's gonna cover the whole place up. The biggest pie you ever saw. There's my pie. And now I'm gonna cut it up in little pieces and share it with all the people. We'll all eat it now.

T: It's time to leave now, Carol.

C: G'by.

T: Good-by, Carol. It's been very nice knowing you.

Discussion: Play Sessions Sixteen through Twenty-one

These sessions are characterized mainly by Carol's exploration of the positive feelings within herself toward herself and other people. She builds a music house with blocks, where children are close to their parents, play games with them, and have fun with them. She makes the house a spacious one, and "the kids are gonna have a good time."

Carol describes her fears of animals and loud noises and recognizes that they are foolish. In her play she shares her pie reluctantly, because "I've been starving to death."

In the twentieth session Carol creates a village in the sand. She decides not to destroy the homes this time and realizes that "if I helped them, then they'd like me." She makes a huge cake in the sand and decides at first to eat it all up, as her "selfish" feelings momentarily return, but later she says, "I'll divide it up with them [all the people], because they're my friends." She now sees herself as a friend, someone whom people care about and regard as important. And in the play experiences Carol indicates that it's not too late, her dreams can still come true.

Finally Carol expresses a very positive friendly attitude toward people, saying, "I'm gonna make a pie so big it's gonna cover the whole place up . . . and now I'm gonna cut it up in little pieces and share it with all the people."

During the therapy experience Carol expressed her deep resentments and fears in her relationship with her mother, using clay and sand to symbolize these attitudes. She was able to talk about her fears that food would be poisoned and also her resentment toward her mother for giving her bad food and so little love. After she had expressed her feelings that she had been cheated and deceived, the food for her was no longer a source of anxiety. It now held a more realistic place in her total life situation. As Carol clarified and reorganized these attitudes toward herself, she became more accepting of herself and her mother. Acceptance of herself and her mother enabled Carol, then, to move out of her inner world and express feelings of affection and friendliness toward others. Many of these positive feelings and explorations were dramatized in her play in the sand. Following the fifteenth play session these socialized attitudes were most clearly revealed. In her play Carol expressed a desire to help people, to do things for them and with them, and to win their friendship and their love. Carol's perceptions of herself and others were now both more positive and more realistic. Her mother's perceptions of Carol were also different.

In the therapist's first contact with the mother, the mother described Carol as selfish, inconsiderate, disagreeable, and unruly. Quoted statements from the therapist's last contact with the mother revealed new attitudes. "It is not very difficult to see Carol's growth. For a long time now we have had to punish her very little. Her manners are improving. She just seems to do things much better. She seems to just get along better with everyone. . . . My husband says she's been acting a lot smarter and has noticed lately that she's using big words when she speaks. . . . I think sometimes when I look at some other people's children that Carol is almost perfect. . . . For four years of her life Carol showed us very little affection, but in the last six months she has begun to kiss us and to hug us. My husband is much warmer to her now, and he spends much more time with her. . . . Last night she said, 'Dear God, please don't let there be any more trouble between my mommy and daddy,' so it shows that she does have a great deal of consideration for us."

CHAPTER VI

Play Therapy with a Preschool Family

It is important in every contact with parents to effectively communicate attitudes of faith, acceptance, and respect. Whether the request for child therapy has come from an agency or from a parent himself, the request is honored in the way it is made. If the parent believes that the child is the cause of life's miseries, this interpretation is accepted. If the parent is completely bewildered about an unnatural turn of events in the child's behavior, such as the sudden occurrence of terrifying fears and nervous tantrums, this feeling is respected. If a parent believes he is completely responsible, at the root of all the trouble, then this attitude is accepted. It is the parent's own immediate perception, then, which is focused upon in the interviews. The therapist attempts to understand, clarify, and open new avenues of awareness and relationship. In these early meetings it is important that the therapist flow with the action as the parent sees it and not create an oppositional force.

Faith in the parent's ability to grow in understanding and accepting his child and in living fully, happily, with him is conveyed to the parent throughout every contact.

No pressure of any kind is put on parents to push them into coming for therapeutic help. The only requirement is that the parent come for an initial interview. At the beginning of this interview the therapist makes some tentative remark, such as, "I know very little about what brought you here. Could you tell me something about it?" From this point the parent leads the interview, and the therapist follows in whatever direction the parent goes, remaining an empathetic listener and creating an atmosphere of complete acceptance.

Sometimes the parent will begin the interview with a discussion concerning the child and will later in the interview express attitudes about himself. At other times the parent will bring in feelings that some other member of the family is primarily responsible for the child's difficulties. Or the parent may concentrate mainly on an elaboration of the child's symptoms and how they are affecting family living or school relations.

Whatever decision the parent makes is accepted. Whatever analysis or evaluation the parent makes is accepted. At the end of the interview, the time arrangements are completed. Then the following attitude is expressed to the parent: "If you'd like to come in at any time and talk over your experiences with your daughter, or anything else, either on a regular basis or whenever you feel that you want to come, I would be happy to make arrangements to see you."

It is surprising how frequently parents decide to come in for counseling help when a belief in their capacity to make decisions and be responsible for them is communicated. Of ten cases of child therapy handled over a period of nine months, four parents decided to come in regularly for counseling, five decided to come in when they felt a special need for it, and one decided that there was no need to come for counseling. The parents who saw the therapist, either regularly or irregularly, soon spoke mostly of their own personal lives and backgrounds, mentioning the children's problems only occasionally.

Frequently parents request information on their child's progress. Brief tentative evaluations are offered, omitting all personal factors that belong only to the child. Occasionally parents wish to discuss specific difficulties or problems they are having in their relations with their children. The therapist responds primarily to the parent's feelings but gives child development information or support when that is what the parent wants and needs. Information is given tentatively, leaving the evaluation of it and the decision to act upon it to the parent.

In discussing the child's play therapy experiences with parents, permission to record play sessions is requested. The one-way-vision mirror in the playroom is explained to the parent, as well as the fact that a person who records the interviews, and sometimes students in training, are in the observation room. Sometimes parents ask to observe their children from behind the mirror. Here a limit is set, and it is explained that this would violate the goals of therapy, and that it would be unfair to the child, who may express deep feelings about his home and family, to be observed without his knowledge by intimately and emotionally involved parents.

Occasionally a child insists that his mother stay in the playroom with him and refuses to remain except under that condition. In cases of this kind it is important to accept the child's decision and permit the parent to remain in the playroom for the entire first session. If the child will come alone the second time, then this decision is accepted. If, on the other hand, the child insists that his mother be present at every play session, this too is accepted by the therapist. The writer has handled three cases with both mother and child in the room and has found in these cases that having mother and child in the room together did not in any way impede therapeutic movement. As a matter of fact, in some ways it seemed to speed up free emotional expression from both mother and child. The values of having mother and child together in the playroom have been investigated by Axline (1). Her tentative conclusion is that both mother and child gain emotional insight when the therapist maintains a completely accepting relationship with each of them.

To illustrate the interaction of therapy and the values lying within it when all members of the family are being seen by the same therapist, abridged recorded transcriptions are presented in chronological order. Brief discussions of the major issues and attitudes expressed and explored in the play therapy sessions will be presented. The reader is urged to examine the entire case before reaching definite impressions and conclusions.

The role of the therapist in the interviews with the parents was to convey a belief that they were the best authorities in deciding how they should act in the relations with their child. The therapist attempted to convey complete acceptance of their feelings and help them examine and explore the various possibilities in their current and past experiences that might be contributing to the child's difficulties. He attempted to follow completely the parents' perceptions of the problems and encouraged them to discover for themselves ways of dealing with the disturbing behavior.

Therapy With a Preschool Family

Mr. B seemed frightened and distressed as he talked on the phone: "I want to come down and talk to you as soon as possible. It's my little girl Kathy. She suddenly seems to be afraid of things. A month ago she woke up one night with a horrible nightmare, and this continued for three nights in succession. Her fears don't seem to go away. One day her mother read her a story about a chicken falling upside down in the air. She screamed with fear and told her mother to tear up the book and throw it away. Now there are some things in each book which she is quite upset about. She wants them all destroyed. One day Kathy saw a billboard sign and started crying. She was afraid of the picture. She didn't even stop enough to hear her mother explain about the billboard. Then on their way home they saw the same billboard again. Her mother had made a mistake and gone by it a second time. Kathy cried for two and a half hours afterwards. We thought she'd never stop. She wakes up and has nightmares. She is terrified. I want to come down and see what I can do about it, for if it's developing into something, I wouldn't want it to drag too long."

After this telephone conversation arrangements were made to see Mr. B, Mrs. B, and their three-year-old daughter, Kathy. Mr. B saw the therapist four times. He made numerous phone calls both between interviews and after completion of the last interview. Mrs. B also saw the therapist four times. A total of fourteen play sessions were conducted with Kathy. Since Kathy absolutely refused to come to the playroom without her mother, the sessions were conducted with both mother and child in the room, and an attempt was made to establish and maintain a therapeutic relationship with both of them during the play sessions.

As the case progressed, Mrs. B herself encouraged Kathy to make decisions, responded more and more to Kathy's feelings, and apparently accepted her behavior completely.

OCTOBER 25. INTERVIEW WITH FATHER

THERAPIST: Feel free to begin wherever you'd like, Mr. B.

FATHER: Actually, my wife is the one that should be able to talk about it, because she's been with her more. I put her to bed at night. I like to do it, and Kathy doesn't mind it. It seems to us that she has a fear, and naturally she can't tell us, and we can't diagnose it. We're so ignorant we can't handle it.

Let's take last night. She talks for a while. She talks about things to herself. At three o'clock this morning she woke up. I used to be a heavy sleeper. Now I wake up at the slightest sound. She was a preemy and was eight months old and was 3 pounds 4 ounces at birth. She's very healthy, and there is nothing wrong with her. When she woke at three o'clock this morning, we found her whimpering. My wife picked her up and brought her in my bed. We're just completely stymied. After she was in our bed for five minutes, I said to Kathy, "Would you like to go in your own bed?" and she said "No," and I said, "You tell us when you want to go in." We waited, and I asked her again several minutes later. We felt we shouldn't force the issue, because maybe she wanted to be with us more. Finally, she said, "O.K.," and she went into her own bed.

After she was in bed, I said, "I will sleep in the bedroom with you." Kathy didn't fall asleep right away. I was just falling asleep when I heard her say she wanted the bedspread all on her. I tried to explain to her that it was too big in the bed. I got out of bed, because Kathy started to cry again. I held her hand and touched her body, and she kept whimpering and sniffling. I gave her a little pat on the back, and she sniffed and lied quietly. I stood there and looked at her, and she asked me why I was looking at her. I have noticed several times before when I told her, "If you want to cry I will give you something to cry about," she would stop crying after I patted her. Our pediatrician said she probably had a fear complex. She fell asleep, and when I went to work this morning she was still sleeping.

(*Pause.*) I don't know whether this is normal, farfetched, or what. This billboard deal last Saturday—I want to tell you about it. I had Kathy with me all day. She had told me, "Don't go down ——— Road." No sooner had we turned the corner, and there was a billboard showing a woodpecker pecking on the tree. She immediately told me that I had promised I wouldn't go down that street. She threw herself on me and started to tremble and cry. I held her and tried to explain about it. She kept saying, "Tear it up—get rid of it." I tried to explain it is not our sign, we can't tear it up.

Maybe we shouldn't have gone into detail with it. Maybe we've always gone into too much detail with her. If I were to tell her a story, she would interrupt me and ask why. If I made a definite answer maybe she wouldn't go any further. After I talked to her, she finally calmed down to some extent. I said, "There is probably some people who own the sign," and I said, "Maybe we can see them and ask about it." Then she smiled. As we went down ——— Road, she said, "Don't go that way." It all ended up where she forgot about it, and we went to my cousin's house, and that was the end of that. Now, Doc, tell me what I should do to get rid of that fear.

T: It isn't anything you *should* do. I mean there are no suggestions I could make. However, perhaps if we continue to talk this out, it may become clearer. Also, if you'd like, Kathy could come here for play therapy sessions, which will give her an opportunity to fully express herself in her own way.

F: Now that doesn't make any sense to me. I came here so you would tell me what to do.

T: And I'm telling you that there isn't anything that you should do.

F: Well, there must be someone I can go to who will tell me what I should do.

T: You want me to just say to you, "Do so-and-so, and so-and-so, and so-and-so." Is that it?

F: Well, not exactly, but I do want you to tell me what to do.

T: Well, there isn't anything that you should do, but we could approach the whole business together if you would tell me some more about your relationships with Kathy.

F: The first time I noticed this fear was when my wife was reading a story to her. She noticed a duck falling, and she became terrified about it. She said, "Take it away—tear it up," and my wife took the book and threw it out. Then Kathy seemed to be satisfied, but later she asked, "Did you throw it out?" That was the end of that incident.

During the day she plays well. So you see, we just don't understand. I know you can't solve this in five minutes' time, but still there must be something that you can tell me to do.

T: You've reached the point where you just can't handle it any more.

F: It might have come on a long time before, like when I took her to the zoo when she was two. We were standing in front of the animal cage, the tiger, and she was trembling, and I walked away at that time. Before that, we used to live on ——— Avenue. Next door there was a little girl older than Kathy. Kathy looked up to her, but this girl treated Kathy very mean. Another time Kathy went to take a dog, and the dog snapped at her.

When we go out for a ride, I suggest we sit together, and we do many things together. We sing together, and so forth. As a matter of fact, Kathy has learned the words to all the popular songs. We live a fairly normal life. We have a home. I have a secure position. We don't bicker. If there is a disagreement, we'll hang off until Kathy is in bed asleep. (Pause.) I have an idea that I should have stopped at the billboard and walked up to it with her and then say to her, "Touch the bird." Any intelligent person will know whether that's right or wrong. (Pause.) I hit her last night, because I thought she was just fooling around.

T: You felt that maybe she was just trying to irritate you, and you were angry.

F: You hit on a point there. Kathy doesn't let a thing pass. She is a very sensitive child. You just touch her, and boom—tears. Maybe I show anger where I am not supposed to. She can read every angle on my face.

    I wish you would talk to Dee. My wife is very easygoing —a patient woman. I would trust her with my child more than any other woman on earth. To me, she is a very good mother. Maybe she could throw some light on all this.

T: You feel she might help us to understand the difficulty a little better.

F: I was here at two-thirty, though I knew the appointment wasn't till three. This was silly, and yet I had to get away from work, with the thought or feeling, "Maybe I am doing something wrong."

T: You feel that you might be to blame for it, then.

F: For one thing, at the supper table the food is on the plate. Once in a while Kathy will want a different plate. If she is wearing a yellow dress, then she wants a yellow plate. If she is wearing a blue dress, then she wants a blue plate, or maybe it's the color of her ribbon that will decide which kind of plate she wants. I decided you've got to be firm and definite, so I said, "Kathy, you will have it in this plate, and you will eat it in this plate or you won't eat it at all."

T: There are some things that she's just got to accept, is that it?

F: She's got to learn to accept that fact. (*Long pause.*) If my own life means anything—. My real mother died when I was born, and I was placed in an orphanage at the insistence of my stepmother. My father remarried shortly after my mother died. Seeing that, my grandmother couldn't see me staying there, so she took me to live with her. I hadn't seen my parents or brothers and sisters at all. Then when I was twelve, my sister suddenly came and got me from my grandmother's, and then I lived with them.

    I can remember a couple of instances when I was terrified. My two uncles had an argument over which way to paint the side of the house. One uncle wanted to fight it out, and I can remember sitting on the curb just frightened, seeing them fight it out.

My stepmother, not being too intelligent and not able to read, favored my sister and more or less didn't care about me. There was such a complete change from my grandmother's home that I was practically alone. I felt that I wasn't wanted. It seems to me that I have felt very insecure most of my life, but I married someone who has all the love and kindness for me and who gives me everything I need, yet I'm not really happy.

T: In spite of your present setup, you still feel insecure.

F: I feel safe to say that I am pretty well set in my life. Going from me to Kathy about that insecurity, maybe I am transferring it to Kathy. When I come home at night I pick her up and kiss her. I ask her how she is and kiss and hug her. When I do that, maybe I speak in too rough a tone, and she may be afraid. I don't know whether it is a feeling of sorrow or a feeling that I wish it could be done away with.

T: I gather you aren't too sure whether you feel sorry or consider it a weakness in her.

F: What's disturbing me is the fact that she's got the fear, and maybe it's deep basically.

T: You're afraid it might be deeper than just the fear she shows.

F: Maybe I should be, but I'm not.

T: In other words, it's the fear that you're most concerned about at this time.

F: I bear her in my mind every moment of the day, and it bothers me. How should we act with a situation like this? It's interfering with my work.

T: It's really been upsetting to you.

F: You could tell me how to handle particular incidents.

T: You want me to tell you what to do.

F: I don't understand her mind like you do. You could tell me what to do.

T: I know you want very much for me to tell you what to do, but what I've been trying to say to you is that there is nothing that you should do.

F: But could you see Kathy? What did you call it? Play something?

T: Yes, I could make some appointments to see Kathy for play therapy sessions. I would suggest that you tell her that she's coming here to play. I would also like to make an appointment with your wife before Kathy comes in.

F: You know, I can't remember a single thing that you've said to me, but somehow I feel better than I did when I came in.

OCTOBER 30. INTERVIEW WITH MOTHER

T: You can feel free to begin wherever you'd like, Mrs. B.

M: I am sure Kathy doesn't know how it affects me. I will tell you what I remember. Just yesterday I was driving down the street, and we saw these sign boards. The eyes bother her all the time. One is a fruit, and there is a big eye on it. She throws herself down in fright. I try to avoid it, but she always finds it.

The other night she watched singing on TV. It was a Halloween program. There was a fire and a ghost in it. We turned the set off as soon as the fire and ghost appeared, but she saw it and she talked six hours afterwards about it. We took her to the dime store, and she saw masks. Now we can't go in the dime store any more.

Now I have to sleep in the room with her, or my husband does. Another thing, she is afraid of the dark. (*Pause.*) She used to be daddy's girl. I don't know what happened. One night they were lying down and he had his back to her, and something happened, and ever since then she feels that way.

T: You can't remember exactly what happened, but you feel that that was quite an important incident.

M: I just can't remember what took place that night. She loves him. She kisses him. Since this stuff started she doesn't behave as well as she used to. She is very negative. She used to sit down and read books for hours. She used to sit down and enjoy the books. She's afraid of the "Big Bad Wolf." She now won't look at her books. One by one she rejected all her records. First it was the "Big Bad Wolf," but then it generalized to everything.

Here's something else. We moved to a new neighborhood, and the girl next door is quite aggressive. My daughter is a big girl, and if she ever kicked someone, they'd really get hurt. We finally got her so when someone hit her, she would hit back. But now it gets to the point where she often starts the hitting, and sometimes she'll want to fight all the time.

She is indefinite about things. If I offer her a sucker, she'll say, "The green one—no, the red one—no, the orange one" and keeps changing her mind, so I offer her two. Do you think that's all right?

Another thing, I don't know if this is unusual. She had a favorite blanket. One day she kept saying, "What's this? What's this?" It was a label on the blanket. About three days after that, she said she didn't want the blanket any more. That's the first thing that she said she didn't want. The other day she said she would use the blanket after the label was taken off, so I cut the label off. We're in a quandary. I don't know whether I should curb her or whether I should just let her do it.

She loves fur. This is something else. She wanted me to buy this fur muff. The thing had two tails on it. She told me I would have to take the tails off. I had to cut the tails off before she would use it. Anything she doesn't want— "Tear it up—I don't want it—get rid of it."

She's not too shy. She knows all the popular songs. She always tells us to tell her kitty (the muff) what she doesn't like to hear herself.

I can't go on ——— Road. I can hardly go anywhere. She looks for it. She's under the strain because of the sign. It isn't the sign. It must be something else. If she sees anyone with their eyes closed, she becomes frightened. If someone closes their eyes to think, then she doesn't like it.

I know the signs and not going to bed drive us crazy. She used to like the dark. I put the night light in her room. She used it about two weeks and was crazy about it. One night, she sobs to herself when she wakes up and doesn't find us there. She'll hold us real tight after we come in but not tell us what it is. The other night we took her into bed, and after she was in it a while I said, "You have to go in your room now." I turned her bed around so it would be parallel to mine. She talked about the train, which was really a reflection from her night light. She is afraid of reflections. While lying on our bed she saw a reflection from the bathroom light. She keeps yelling on and on and on, "Take it away!" I had to throw the night light away. She used to say, "I don't like that. Give it to Donna. I don't like the night lamp. Give it to Donna."

I've reached a point where I don't know whether it is me, whether it is a playmate, or who it is. Once I had a re-hearsal, and my husband had to work. We left a sitter. We came back, and Kathy was just scared. Frankly, we don't leave her too much. My husband is afraid to leave her with anyone. The first sitter was about six months ago. Kathy is terrified continually when she has free time. Then when she's playing with her playmates she doesn't mention it. The minute she sits down to relax, then she starts talking about it. Lately she has wanted me to feed her.

Let me ask you something. As far as my husband's home-life and mine, we never fight. We never argue in front of our daughter. I never nag. If he wants to go out bowling or someplace, then he goes. There is never any argument. We never bicker or argue. But there must be something. Maybe she could be jealous about our relationship. (*Pause.*)

As soon as we saw this TV show, she saw fire and masks and eyes. She doesn't miss a thing. We tried to shut it off before she could see it, but she saw it anyway. It couldn't be just eyes. Her being afraid of the night light means she's not afraid of just eyes. There was a chicken falling in the air in one of her books, and that frightened her, and that has noth-ing to do with eyes.

Our daughter means the whole world to us—both of us. Apparently we do something wrong. We do feel that it is probably us, but I can't see it. Nothing has changed. I guess we've drawn the conclusions that it is always the parents from what people tell us. My sister-in-law voiced the opin-ion that we were teaching her too much. She's such a well-spoken child. Could she be angry because everyone tells me how good she is?

T: Evidently you feel that might anger her.

M: Suddenly it occurred to me that this is possible. When we go out, she performs better than anyone else. We went to a birthday party just a while ago. She sang a number of songs and entertained the people. We always have felt proud of her. We compliment her a lot. I read someplace to tell the child it was well done. Maybe she has too much of a strain on her.

T: You mean you might expect too much of her.

M: If I understood what it was, I could fight it. If it were one of us, we would try to correct it.

T: You would be willing to change if you thought it would help.

M: I try to change the subject when she starts talking about it, but she's too smart and comes right back to the fear that she was describing.

T: She is very persistent then.

M: Let me ask you something. I took many of the TV programs that she used to watch away. The pediatrician said "Howdy Doody" is all right. Would you let her watch that? We figured it wouldn't harm her to see these programs, but it does. Just an innocent program might frighten her.

She is perfectly fit physically, and now we have to have this thing on us. She doesn't go into tantrums when she is terrified. She just whimpers and sobs quietly. Something else—if she is doing something and you touch her the wrong way, she gets real tense, and she'll say, "Put it back."

Sunday we thought we'd take her out to the park. She got up on the slide and went down a couple of times without any difficulty. Then the third time the girl in front and the girl behind began to push, and she was caught between them. I yelled to my husband to get up there and get her, and he shouted to Kathy to come on down the slide. Kathy was absolutely terrified. She couldn't move. So finally my husband reached up and got her. After that incident maybe there was some connection with my husband. Maybe it is him, because she wouldn't let him push her on the swing. She wanted me to push her.

Everything must be just right for her. My cousin gave me a blue skirt for Kathy. I tried it on my daughter, and now she wears that skirt continually. She won't put anything else on. I washed the skirt, and even before I have it ironed she wants to put it on. She has all kinds of dresses and skirts and slacks, but all she asks for is that blue skirt. She won't wear her royal blue dress. She won't wear slacks any more.

The mother next door took the easy way out and stuck her daughter in our yard. I would always have to put her in their yard, because she would get into such a fight with Kathy. Do you think it is the lack of playmates? Kathy is selfish with her toys, too, but then all children her age are. Yesterday she wanted a piece of gum. I broke it in two and gave her half. I wanted to give the other half to a boy who was riding with her. Kathy screamed and shouted that she wanted the whole stick. Fortunately the boy's daddy had gum with him and gave the boy a piece. Her daddy took the other half. She yelled and cried just like a spoiled brat. I figured, "Let her cry it out." Her dad was just about to interfere with it when I cautioned him to leave her alone. She told me to throw it away. Finally she ended up by chewing half a stick.

T: In other words, when you insisted on maintaining this limit, she was finally able to accept it.

M: I let her know when she's done something wrong. I really believe there is something in the relation with my husband. Now she doesn't want her daddy to put her to sleep. She wants me to do it. If I'm not there, though, she'll cling to her dad. If he can get her in the right mood even now, she'll let him put her to sleep. When he picks her up now, she tenses. Her daddy—whenever she does something, he wants her to do it just right. Her daddy always tells her what to do. She'll say, "No, I want to do it like this." Then he leaves her alone. I don't notice that he's done that so much. I just happened to notice it just yesterday. He calls me forty times a day. After he talked to you, he was fine. He is being exceptionally sweet to her. No child could want a better daddy. He doesn't correct her too much.

We're never relaxed any more. After she goes to sleep at night we sit in the living room, and even the slightest stir from her bedroom makes us feel very uneasy. We just seem to wait for her to stir. Another thing, we haven't been giving her naps. She hasn't done so for about a half a year. She was terrified—either I sleep in her room or she doesn't sleep. She is keeping it in to herself all the time. When she wakes up she'll sob quietly—just lies there pitifully but doesn't try to call to us.

What do we do when my husband and I don't agree on the treatment of something? It happened yesterday, but I can't remember exactly what the incident was. However, sometimes when she wants to eat out of a blue dish rather than the one I've set before her, or if she wants a flower glass, then I'll get her that. Should I do these things? My husband doesn't think so, but I don't think it makes any difference. What do you think about it?

T: Evidently you get somewhat worried when your husband disagrees with you.

M: My husband and I have been married nine years, and we have never really quarreled. We just don't do it. Everything has been wonderful. We never argue in front of Kathy, though if I do something that he thinks is wrong, he tells me about it in a way that she doesn't know about it, but maybe she has understood all these times and we didn't know it. Maybe she has been sensitive to this. Tell me—will you be able to correct these fears?

T: That's something that is really troubling you. There is no definite way I can answer that. It will depend on whether or not Kathy and I can work out the kind of relationship that will enable her to express herself freely.

M: What time should I bring Kathy in?

T: Would one-thirty on Wednesday be all right?

M: Yes, that would be fine.

T: If you would like to come in yourself, either regularly or from time to time, just to talk things over, you can let me know.

M: Right now I can't tell you. I still don't feel too good about this whole thing, but if I decide that I want to come and see you, it probably will only be from time to time.

November 1. Play Session with Kathy

T: (*Shows Kathy the bathroom.*)

C: I'm not thirsty.

T: You can use these things any way you like.

C: (*Walks into room with T, then runs back into hall to get mother. Mother sits on chair and C runs out to hall again. Carries in small chair.*)

T: Kathy wants to bring in her own chair.

C: (*Looks at mother while holding chair.*)

M: Put it down.

C: I wanta make toys, Mama. (*Picks up truck.*) Mama, how do you work this?

T: Kathy wants Mama to tell her how to work it.

C: What's this, Mama?

M: That's a dish.

C: Here. (*Hands mother a ball, balloon, dish, and truck.*)

T: Kathy just wants Mama to have everything.

C: (*Continues giving mother play materials.*)

M: Thank you.

C: This is a hoe. You got a hoe. I like the hoe. (*Hands mother a tractor.*) Here, Mama. (*Pulls chair closer to table and sits down.*) A boat. A hot water bottle, if I wanta. (*Picks up gun.*) This is a gun. (*Looks at T and continues to handle toys. Picks up telephone.*) What's this? (*Hands mother a rubber knife.*) Here's a knife for you. That's a sharp one.

M: Mm-hm.

T: You want her to have a sharp one.

C: You can cut, Mama. (*Handles the gun again.*) Here's a gun. Here, Mama. Lookit this gun and shoot. (*Hands gun to mother.*) You shot me.

M: I shot you?

C: Yeah. (*Kathy takes gun and shoots mother. Hands T the little miniature gun.*)

T: You want me to have this one, hm? O.K.

C: Now quiet. I'm gonna talk. (*Holds large telephone and turns dial a few times.*) I'm dialing and dialing. Hello. Hello. Who's there? Mama, you use this one and I'll use that one. (*Hands mother large telephone and takes smaller one for herself.*) What's this, Mama?

M: It's a steam shovel.

C: What does it do?

M: It picks up dirt.

C: (*Handles telephone again.*) I'm gonna call up. Hello? Who's there? Nobody's there. (*Replaces telephone on table.*) Here's an airplane, Mama. It flies.

M: Mm-hm.

C: And here's an automobile. And another car. (*Moves to doll furniture and doll figures.*) Here, doll. Sit on the couch. Another doll. Look, Mama. She's got her pajamas on, Mama.

M: Mm-hm.

C: Here's a bed. (*Continues to handle doll furniture. Picks up washstand and examines it. Handles part of the steam shovel. Looks at cat balloon on floor and then at mother. Picks up balloon and carries it to mother.*) This is a heavy balloon.

T: A real heavy one.

C: See what color it is. What color?

M: Purple.

C: Purple. (*Gives mother the balloon.*) Here's another balloon.

T: You want Mama to have all the balloons. Just piling them all up on her.

C: Fly the balloons up in the air.

M: I can't. My hands are full.

T: Kathy wants Mama to fly the balloons in the air, but Mama can't.

C: (*Picks up small washing machine.*) What's this?

M: You know what that is.

C: It goes around and around. Turn it.

M: I can't. My hands are full.

C: (*Hands T the washing machine.*) Will you do it?

T: It's very hard to turn, isn't it? There.

C: (*Holds washing machine. Sits next to blocks and handles a few of them. Goes to doll furniture and picks up rubber doll.*) Take the diaper off and wash it.

M: I can't. Ask Mr. C if he will help you.

C: I'll stick myself with the pins.

T: Is that what you're afraid of?

C: Yes.

T: (*Removes pin from doll's diaper.*)

C: (*Places diaper in washing machine.*) Make it wash.

M: Honey, I can't. I'm too loaded down.

C: (*Places washing machine on floor.*) It's washing.

T: It's finally washing, and you're getting it all clean.

C: (*Sighs heavily. Sits on floor and watches washing machine.*) It's turning.

T: Mm-hm.

C: Around and around and around.

T: That's the way it goes.

C: (*Looks at large comeback toy.*) What's over there with the hands?

T: What do you suppose that could be, Kathy?

C: (*Goes to comeback and lifts it.*)

T: Boy, you could lift it right up.

C: (*Carries comeback around floor to mother. Places it in front of her. Goes back to washing machine.*) Look, Mama. It's washing. It's gotta get dry 'cause it's dirty. Now stand over and let it wash. (*Picks up bells from table.*) Jingle, jingle, jing. Jingle, jingle, jing. (*Picks up miniature hammer.*) Mama, this is a hammer. What do you hammer on?

T: On anything you want to.

C: I can hammer on—so. (*Hammers on bells.*) Is there a big hammer down here?

M: I don't know.

C: Who wants to hammer? Who wants to hammer? (*Hands T the hammer.*)

T: You think I want to have that.

C: Here's a gun. (*Hands mother the gun. Picks up small doll.*) Baby gonna go swimming. That's what I was looking for.

T: You want the baby to go swimming.

C: What's this, Ma? (*Small balloon.*)

M: It's a little balloon.

C: How did it get little?

M: I don't know.

C: You can have that balloon.

M: Thank you.

C: You can have the pretty balloon. (*Hands balloon to T.*) What fell? (*Gives mother blue gun that has fallen from her arms. Picks up small nursing bottle.*) Here, Mama. For you. And I'll take the big bottle.

T: You'll take the big bottle and Mama will have the little one.

C: Is there a doll I can feed, Mama?

M: Look around and see if there is.

T: You want one you can feed.

M: How about that one by Mr. C?

C: (*Picks up rubber doll, places it in her lap, and feeds it with large bottle of water.*) Now drink. Is the water coming out? I need a big baby, Mama. I need a big baby. I really need a big baby. I need a real heavy baby. I've got a big bottle.

T: You need a heavy baby.

C: I need a big baby. I gotta have a big baby—a heavy one. Mama, is there one like that?

M: I don't know.

C: I'm looking for another one. Mama, is there any big ones down here?

M: Well, find something to feed.

T: Kathy wants her mother to find her a big baby, and mother just can't.

C: I need a big baby. Mama, I gotta feed a big baby.

T: You just have to.

C: Mama, I gotta have a big baby.

M: Well, I just can't help you, honey.

T: Kathy just needs a big one.

C: I'll feed this one. (*Places small rubber doll in lap again.*) Now drink your bottle. Now drink your bottle. (*Glances at diaper in washing machine.*) It's washing. Look. Diaper's washing. Maybe I better put some water in it. (*Takes diaper out of machine and pours water into it. Covers it again.*) It's got to wash. It's got to wash.

T: It's got to get clean.

C: (*Handles doll and bottle again.*) She's got to drink it. She's got to.

T: She's just got to drink it.

C: Her diaper's washing, Mama.

M: Mm-hm.

C: I'll get all wet. There's water in there. Why doesn't the water come out?

T: You're wondering why it doesn't come out.

C: Why doesn't the water come out, Mama? It's supposed to. She changed her mind and she wants to have the other bottle. Give me the other bottle. (*Takes small bottle from mother. Feeds doll with small bottle.*) It doesn't come out, Mama.

M: It doesn't?

C: No.

T: It just stays in the bottle and won't come out.

C: Can I take it off? (*Nipple.*) Mama, how do you open that big thing? How do you open it? This kind of open is easy. (*Refers to small nipple.*) Mama, why does it stay in the bottle? I want it to feed.

T: You want it to be fed.

C: Feed it. She almost drinks the water up.

M: (*Laughs.*)

C: Oooooh. Look what happened. Look what happened. (*Looks surprised at water that has dripped on her thighs.*)

M: That's O.K., honey. You can dry in the car.

C: If I get my dress wet, I can wear my slacks?

M: Yes, you can.

C: Oh, it got on my slip. I'm not getting it on the chair any more. Drink it all up. Can you pour some more water into this bottle? Can you pour some more water in here? My mama's hands are too full. (*Hands T large bottle. Takes nipple off small bottle herself.*)

T: Let's see. (*Loosens nipple from large bottle.*)

C: (*Transfers some water from large bottle to small one.*) Gotta put the top on. Quick! Before I spill it. It's too much.

T: There's too much in there.

C: Quick! Before I spill. (*Replaces nipple on small bottle.*) Now she's got some more water. She wanted some more and now she's got more. She's real thirsty. Boy oh boy.

T: You like to feed the baby.

C: Yes. She almost drank the water out. See? (*Shows mother the washing machine.*) It's dirty.

T: It's getting washed just like you wanted it to. (*Pause.*) Kathy, you only have a short while longer to play today.

C: Did you see what happened? It got all wet. Mama, do you have another pair of clothes for me?

M: I've got blue jeans or slacks in the car.

C: Blue jeans. You want to put all those things down. I'll help you. (*Unloads items from mother's arms.*) I'm gonna cut. (*Picks up knife.*) Mama, what should I cut?

M: Look around for something to cut.

C: I don't see any crust.

M: I don't think there is any bread down here. (*To T:*) She doesn't like the crust on her bread, so we've been cutting it off, but lately she's been eating it. (*To Kathy:*) Don't you, honey?

C: I'm gonna cut some bread and butter. (*Gets into sandbox and plays with sand.*)

T: We have to leave now. Next week is your time again.

M: We'll come back again, honey.

T: This time will be saved for Kathy each week.

C: (*Gets out of sandbox. Walks out of room with mother and T, with a backward glance at the room.*)

Discussion: November 1 Play Session

Kathy clings to her mother for a short while. She proceeds to load her mother down with toys and playthings. Kathy wishes to express angry feelings toward her mother. She would like to shoot her with a toy gun but is able to do this only after enticing the mother into shooting her first. Kathy continues to load her mother. Even when the mother protests, "I can't. My hands are full," Kathy continues pressing her mother to hold more and more toys. Kathy shows general restlessness in her hyperactive movements and anxiety in the constant questions to the mother. She wants the mother to do everything for her and frustrates her mother by loading her down and then asking her to do things. Kathy seems to feel hostile toward her mother but is unable to express these feelings directly.

Kathy is uncomfortable and unsettled in the playroom. She doesn't seem to know what she wants to do and moves about from one toy to another. She avoids the therapist almost completely yet is very aware of his presence.

Kathy finally decides to do something, to feed the baby, and exclaims, "I need a big baby, Mama." Kathy, for the first time, begins to play with continuity and persistence. There is considerable emphasis on cleanliness, as Kathy scrubs the baby's diaper again and again and shouts to the therapist "It's got to wash. It's got to wash." There is a compulsive quality in feeding the baby, "She's got to drink it. She's got to."

In a number of instances Kathy expects the mother to respond immediately to her demands and becomes angry when there is a delay, talking louder and louder. Toward the end of the session Kathy gets a little water on her slip. She becomes upset, asks for another set of clothes, and seems worried about being unclean.

November 8. Play Session with Kathy

C: (*Runs into room and looks at toys on table.*)

T: Well, here we are now.

C: (*Picks up chair and carries it to table. Sits down and handles canoe.*) Here's a boat. Here's a boat. One for you. (*Hands T a boat.*) And here's a boat for you, Mommy.

T: You know just what you want to give me and what you want to give your mommy.

C: Here, Mommy. No more. What's that? (*Picks up canoe paddle.*)

M: What does it look like? It looks like a canoe paddle.

C: I wanta play in the sand. (*Steps into sandbox and sits on ledge with feet in the sand. Plays with steam shovel in sand.*)

T: It shovels right in there.

C: Mommy, I'm gonna make you a cake.

M: O.K.

C: First a pie. Down, down, down. Downtety down. Down, down, downtety down. Down, down, downtety down.

T: You just want it to stay down.

C: Down, down, downtety down. Mommy, I got myself dirty. (*Rubs hard at hands.*)

M: That's all right.

C: I brush myself off. (*Goes to table and picks up a gun.*) Here's a gun like Donna's.

M: Mm-hm.

C: Shoot me with it. (*Hands gun to mother, who shoots.*)

T: Bang. Mommy shot you with the gun, just like you wanted her to.

C: (*Returns to sandbox. Hums.*) Here's yours. I made it already. Here.

M: Thank you.

C: Now eat it, Mommy.

M: O.K.

C: I'll wait till you're finished eating it. Are you all finished?

M: Mm-hm.

C: Mommy, the last time I played with water, and I got all wet.

M: Mm-hm.

C: Here. Eat it. (*Hands T a dish filled with sand.*) Are you all finished?

T: I'm all finished.

C: Give it to me. (*Pulls chair close to sandbox. Sits down and dangles feet over sandbox. Reaches down into sandbox for sand and grunts.*) You're gonna get this one.

T: It really is hard to do, isn't it?

. . . . .

C: Mommy's gonna get the green boat. Now Mommy's gonna get it.

T: Mommy's going to get it.

C: Yes. You had yours.

T: I had mine and that's all.

C: I just gotta have one once a day.

T: One once a day. That's all you need.

C: Yes. (*Hands mother boat filled with sand and watches her pretend to eat.*) What do you got in your mouth? Lunch?

M: Mm-hm.

C: Now here. You can eat from it.

T: You want me to eat from it, too.

C: That's enough. Once a day.

T: Once a day is all you need.

C: (*Moves chair to table with toys.*) Mommy, sing "Red Red Robin."

M: You sing it, honey.

C: No, you sing it. (*Jingles bells while mother sings.*) Here's one for you. And you jingle that one. (*Hands a bell to mother and one to T.*) You jingle that. (*Goes to sandbox.*) I'm gonna make you a little jungle-ungle things.

T: You're going to make jungle-ungle things.

C: First I gotta get it all set. Here. Here's your jungle things. What's that for? (*Bells.*) Where did you get it? Over here?

M: You gave it to me.

C: I gave it to you. Why?

M: I don't know.

C: It's gotta go with the kitty. Well, well. (*Moves from sandbox. Goes to dollhouse and furniture.*) Where's the washing machine? I can't find it.

T: Where did that washing machine go?

C: What's this?

M: What does it look like?

C: A washing machine.

T: Kathy just wants Mommy to tell what everything is.

C: Where's the baby's diaper? Mommy, where's the baby's diaper?

M: Look for it, honey.

C: (*Looks in dollhouse.*) Where's the washing machine? Oh, here. Oh, I wish there was a fire. You better not go near there 'cause there's a fire. (*Shoots gun down the chimney of dollhouse.*)

T: You're really going to shoot it down. Bang, bang, bang.

C: Shoot down this one. This mommy doll. She'll be burned by a real hot fire.

T: She'll be burned by a real hot fire.

C: (*Goes back to doll furniture and picks up toy lamp shade.*) Look! A lamp shade. This can go in there, too. (*Drops shade into sandbox.*)

T: Something else goes in there.

C: This can go in there, too. (*Drops bells into sandbox.*)

T: Mm-hm.

C: Mommy, I gotta wash that now. Where's the baby's diaper? Gotta wash it. Unpin it. (*Hands doll with diaper to mother.*)

T: You want Mommy to unpin it.

M: I'll unpin it and you pull it out.

C: Take it out. Here. Hold it. Mommy, I want this to wash. Make it wash.

T: You want it to be really clean.

C: Yes. This will go around and around and wash. (*Stuffs diaper into washing machine.*) It washes. It didn't wash good. It didn't wash good. Gotta look for another diaper. No more, I think. (*Looks over pile of doll furniture.*) Here's a toilet in case baby has to go make. Open it for the baby. (*Places baby doll on toy toilet.*) Baby make sissy. She's making sissy. She's making sissy. (*Places doll on stairway of dollhouse.*) Go right on the steps. Make it right on the steps.

T: You want her to go right on the steps.

C: Baby's gotta make.

T: She has to make.

C: Wash and wash. Diaper isn't dry yet. Put some sand in here. Put some sand in here. (*Pours some sand into washing machine.*) Gotta wash. Get washed and dried. Clean up. (*Empties washing machine over sand box. Bangs the washer against side of sandbox to remove all the sand.*) No more. Gonna wash now. It's gonna wash now. Gonna wash.

T: Your time is up for today now.

C: Mommy, will you read me a story before we go? Read me a story.

M: O.K.

C: Hold my hand.

T: You want Mommy to hold your hand real tight.

Discussion: November 8 Play Session

Kathy's great concern about keeping clean reappears. She looks at her hands and becomes upset, seeing sand on them. She rubs hard at her hands until every speck of sand is removed. Cleanliness anxiety has been Kathy's most clearly expressed negative attitude up to this point. Her hostility toward her mother has been vague and very tentative.

Kathy begins to respond more to the therapist, moving back and forth from her mother to the therapist, giving him things to hold and making things for him. She shows her hostility, too, by asking the adults to eat sand.

Kathy's repetitive anxious questioning continues. In the play the hostility toward the mother now becomes more direct. She runs to the dollhouse, shoots down the chimney, and expresses anger against the mother doll, shouting, "Shoot down this one. This mommy doll. She'll be burned by a real hot fire."

Kathy searches for the "baby's diaper" and yells to her mother, "Mommy I gotta wash that now . . . gotta wash it."

She shows immaturity, placing the baby doll on the stairway of the dollhouse and saying, "She's making sissy. Go right on the steps. Make it right on the steps." Kathy's need to regress in this way is perhaps motivated by a need to escape the everyday pressures directing her toward rapid maturity.

At the end of the session Kathy mixes water and sand, becomes anxious on seeing the dirty water and walks over and holds her mother's hand.

NOVEMBER 13. INTERVIEW WITH MOTHER

M: There are a million things I want to ask you. Her adenoids are very bad. They wake her up almost every night. She just lays there and can't breathe, and it terrifies her. One of us will try to quiet her, and it takes about two hours to quiet her. Will it hurt to have her adenoids taken out at this time? I haven't called the pediatrician yet to tell him. Her lips are continually sore and cracked.

She didn't get to bed until three o'clock last night. One of us has to stay with her every evening. She is terrified with everything in her bedroom. Now what can I do about it? I can just see the terror in her face. Finally I asked her what was bothering her, and she said she didn't want the linoleum in her room. But I don't think that's the solution, because then she wants something else destroyed. She made me paste something over the decal. Yesterday I had to cover up another one. She said she didn't like the animals in it. When she has to go to bed she is just terrified.

The day I called you to make an appointment we were really desperate. My husband had gone in to her, and he kept saying, "Why are you crying? Why are you crying? Stop it! What's the matter with you?" He is a very good daddy. He is not strict or anything. She wouldn't tell him what was the matter. I walked in and took her, and she came to me immediately. I held her for a while, and then I put her back in bed. My husband didn't sleep all night.

Next morning my husband called, and he heard her sing, "Faraway places, that's where I want you to go." He got the idea that if he went away for a week, things would be better for her, but that night when he came home, she was so friendly to him he changed his mind. Usually he comes home in his work clothes. This time he came home with one of his good shirts, and she liked the shirt he was wearing. She clung to him. She wouldn't have anything to do with me. She insisted on him doing things for her. Everything was fine. Could it be the clothes he's wearing? Yesterday he was all dressed up, but she wouldn't do anything with him. He used to always put her to bed. She always preferred him, I told you.

She got over the sign boards. She doesn't cry any more. She is terrified by other sign boards now, but she doesn't cry like she used to. She just hides until we go by and then jumps up.

T: She acts differently but she's still afraid.

M: I don't know what to do, because she is increasing now. I think my husband should come down and talk with you. But he doesn't want to come. He figures he knows he is doing wrong, and we can't figure it out. He wants somebody to give him more direct replies than you do.

T: He wants to talk to someone who will give him direct answers.

M: (*Pause.*) It's gotten so that we don't agree. The other day her coat was lying on the floor. She wanted me to get her things. He brought it instead. She said to me she wanted me to bring it. He thinks I am catering to her. He doesn't agree with me. I was tickling her with her muff, and she enjoyed it. He considers it catering. He disagrees with me, and he'll make a remark about it.

T: You mean there are some things he doesn't think you should do for her.

M: If I feel like doing it, I do it. But my husband considers it catering. She enjoys it. Of course, he does the same thing, but he doesn't see it. He makes remarks, maybe a little remark here or there, and she'll catch it. It's been killing me, but I don't say anything until she's in bed.

T: You keep it to yourself, then, until Kathy isn't around, although it hurts.

M: If I say something, it's so she can't hear it. Yesterday something happened. She hadn't gone to the bathroom for a while. We never trained her. She trained herself. At nine months she automatically began going herself to the toilet. For the other, she'd hear the older kids say "sissy," so she'd say "sissy," and then I took her to the bathroom. Now in the last four days she's really been resisting. I said, "You haven't gone for four hours. Daddy says you have to go before we leave the house." This was on Sunday. I thought I had tricked her into it. I got her upstairs and asked her to please go. I said, "You're wearing a big blouse like a big girl, so show me that you can go like a big girl." I said, "Don't you think you should go to the bathroom? Then there wouldn't be any trouble." I think there was too much of an issue made of it.

    I feel it must be something that me and my husband are doing. If you could just tell us something—something to do with her. I wanted her to go to bed. Her face—she didn't want to cry. Now there isn't a thing in that room that doesn't terrify her. Let me ask you something else. If when she wakes up at night and she's terrified, would it hurt to take her into bed with us? I don't think that's a solution. I don't know what I've been doing. I've tried all kinds of things.

You know, what's wrong is we never had problems with her before. She always used to go to bed. She used to have a picnic. The books started the fears, then all records, then the signs. The whole process started. Maybe it started before then and I don't know about it.

T: It's just too puzzling.

M: Even up to now we haven't done anything. As far as my husband and I, we haven't changed. Maybe she's now seen something. Is that possible? This is the honest truth—my husband and I never disagree. We've never had a disagreement, never had a fight. We have never really had an argument until a few years ago. We used to take about two hours and pick each other apart about once a month, just for the fun of it. There was never really any criticism—there was so little. I don't know how to explain it. We used to just say, "Get it off your chest." We're very, very compatible. Here's something, though. We do disagree about my daughter now. Like yesterday, she said something about the sign, and he was harsh, and I gave him a look. After we went to bed he said, "You didn't have to look at me like that." I knew he was mad because I looked at him like that. Would you say that my husband and I should make up our minds not to disagree in her presence?

T: Evidently you feel that's what you should do.

M: She is such a darling child. She is so well behaved. She isn't any more. She lets you know when she doesn't like something. It bothers me that maybe it is something that won't be cured. Is that considered something mental? My husband and I are thinking of having another child. He thinks it would help her. She is very, very jealous. If some other child comes over and hangs on to me, she'll push his hand off.

My husband is just waiting for me to talk about Kathy's

play each time she comes. Why is it when she leaves here, nothing registers? Here's what I wanted to know. Should we talk about her play here with her? My husband didn't understand. He said, "What did you do today?" I didn't think he should question her, so I told him it would be better if he didn't. He started to say, "Is that all you did today?" when she answered his question, leaving out her trip here. I changed the subject, and afterwards my husband and I talked it over. Can you ask me questions? Is there anything you want to know? Could it be a trifling thing? (*Pause.*)

I have been trying to make our family life perfect. Mother and Dad didn't get along too well. They used to fight and nag, so I always said I wasn't going to get married. Then when I grew up I said I wouldn't nag and I would always trust my husband. According to my husband, I think I have lived up to it. When he is late for dinner he'll come in and I'll give him a kiss and treat him just the same. I never question him. If he goes to the show with the boys, I would never say, "No, don't go," nor am I mad about it. Everyone who knows me has said I'm a very happy person. We live a perfect married life. I would never tell my husband that he does the wrong things.

T: You're very happy, and so you wouldn't tell him he's wrong, is that it?

M: It couldn't be just my husband, anyway. It could be both of us. Because right now she doesn't like him, he's sure it might be him. On Friday I was just desperate. He was all set to go away for a week to no place at all.

T: You felt quite desperate about that.

M: He heard her singing over the phone, "I wish he'd go away for a week," and so he made a personal connection. But that night maybe she was sorry, because she showed him a lot of attention and affection. She didn't want him to hold her. She'd look away—she wouldn't look at him. The minute I came in, she held on so tight to me. I love her as much as he does, but I get a lot of joy in seeing her make him happy. I like to see her be daddy's girl.

Here's something else I could tell you. When she's doing
something, if he wants her to stop he'll pick her up and
tickle her and tries to get her to forget about it. Now he's
trying to distract her too often, I think. When she is crying
when she's with me, I don't try too hard to get her out of
it. First of all, I don't think it would have hurt to let her
play five more minutes with the toys. Instead of picking
her up and making games out of it, and forcing her to bed,
I would just let her play a little longer.

Here's something else. She always used to go up and
down the steps. Now I've got to hold her hand. She'll stand
there and she'll cry and cry and cry. Most of the time I will
try to make a game of it. (*Pause.*)

T: I see that our time is up for today. Would you like to come
in again next week?

M: Yes.

November 15. Play Session with Kathy

C: (*Runs into room and picks up bells.*) Mama. Mama, what do
you do with this?

M: Anything you want to, honey.

C: Here's another one. Two jingles, two jingles, two jingles.

T: Two jingles up and down.

C: (*Holds bells in lap. Fills dish with sand and pushes bells into
dish. Picks up spoon. Takes bells out of dish and digs in
dish with spoon. Looks at mother.*) How do you use this?

M: Any way you want to.

C: What do you do with it?

M: What would you like to do with it?

C: What you call this?

M: A bowl.

C: What do you do with a bowl? (*Continues to chop at sand with
spoon.*)

T: You'd like to be told exactly how to do things.

C: (*Continues to work with sand and spoon. Spills some sand
on skirt and brushes it off.*) What do you think I'm doing?
I think I'm chopping.

M: Oh, is that what you're doing? What Mommy makes?

C: (*Looks at large comeback toy while fingering sand. Picks up big shovel and hands it to mother.*) Here, Mommy. Here, take this.

M: Mm-hm.

C: (*Continues to chop at sand with spoon.*) You can't get this one, Mama, 'cause I'm chopping with it. (*Puts more sand into dish from sandbox and chops it.*) Mommy.

M: What?

C: You know this yellow chair matches my yellow skirt?

M: Mm-hm.

C: It does. (*Digs at sand in dish. Tries to pull slip down below skirt.*) Mommy, I want my slip to peek out.

M: You want it to peek out? Well, pull it out then.

C: It doesn't peek out, Mama. (*Pulls at slip again.*)

T: Now it just peeks out, hm?

C: I can look at it myself now, Mama.

T: It's peeking out now.

. . . . . .

C: (*Takes small doll from dollhouse. Picks up small bottle from bench and feeds doll. Has mother remove nipple from bottle and then continues to feed doll. Walks around room holding doll and bottle.*) She's drinking a lot of water already. There's no more water, baby. Hurry! Drink it.

T: She's got to drink it in a hurry or she doesn't get any more.

C: Drink the water, baby, or you won't get any more. If she doesn't drink it up, there won't be any more.

T: Nothing else for her if she doesn't do as she's told.

C: You gotta drink this, baby. Drink up. Drink up, baby. Quick! You gotta drink up, baby. (*Stands in front of mother and feeds doll.*) I don't think she's got enough water. There. You know you gotta drink the water. Drink it. She's drinking. Oh, baby! (*Laughs.*) Drink some more. (*Puts doll and bottle on bench. Picks up large bottle and looks at mother.*) Mama, I gotta have a big baby.

T: You've got to have a big one to feed with that, hm?

C: (*Picks up a balloon and holds it.*) You know who's gonna get this one? Mama. Mama, take this one. (*Hands mother the balloon. Pours water from large bottle into washing ma-chine. Places bottle and washer on floor and picks up doll and small bottle. Hands bottle to mother.*) You feed her.

M: All right.

C: (*Holds doll while mother feeds it.*) Look, Mama. My sleeve got wet.

M: It'll dry, honey.

C: It's wet.

M: It'll dry, dear.

T: It got all wet, hm? And you don't like it.

C: Push my sleeve up, Mommy. (*Hands doll to mother.*) Mommy, take the baby.

M: You want me to take it?

C: Take it off. Take the diaper off.

T: You want to tell Mommy just what to do.

C: Gotta wash it now. (*Carries diaper to washing machine. Stuffs it into machine.*)

T: Mm-hm. Washing it in the machine.

C: (*Takes diaper out of machine and dips it into dish with sand. Stuffs it back into washing machine again. Takes it out again and rubs it in sand. Puts it into machine but imme-diately takes it out and puts it back into dish of sand. Pounds at diaper with small hammer. Rubs it in sand again. Looks at mother briefly. Continues to handle sand and diaper.*)

T: I guess that'll be all for today, Kathy. We've got to leave now.

C: (*Looks at T and brushes sand from her hands.*) Mommy, read me one of those magazines.

M: You mean the ones upstairs?

C: Yes, those. (*Walks out of room with mother and T.*)

Discussion: November 15 Play Session

Kathy continues her play in the sand, talks incessantly while playing, and asks her mother a number of questions. She chatters constantly and seemingly diverts her mother while she messes in the sand.

Kathy's attention span, in her play, is now much longer and more concentrated. She still becomes upset when she gets sand on herself and wipes hard at the sand until it is all removed. She feeds the baby doll and repeats frequently that the baby *has* to eat. She reenacts the compulsive washing of the diaper repeatedly, scrubbing it over and over again.

NOVEMBER 16. INTERVIEW WITH FATHER

T: Well, how has everything been going?

F: Look. First time in my life I have started to smoke. This thing has really got me. I have a few reasons why I believe Kathy is anxious and indefinite, saying one thing and then two seconds later saying, "I want this thing." This is probably caused by me for a couple of reasons. For one thing, the incident I told you about picking her up and saying, "We're going to bed." That was when she started having these fears at night. She pushed on my chest and didn't want me to take her. It may have been she didn't want to go up. I pushed her down. I should have treated her more gently. I shouldn't have pushed her so hard.

   Dee tells me she mentions me every day. I believe her. Another incident—when I used to go in the room when she cried to herself it was as if she was holding something back. I would go in and ask her what was wrong. She wouldn't answer—probably she was afraid. It was probably the tone of voice that I used, as if to say, "What the hell are you crying for when it's time to sleep?" When I picked her up and said, "Put your arms around me," she looked at me askance.

T: In other words, you felt that she was drawing away from you.

F: I felt rejected by her. She was looking at me in a certain way as though I had done something terrible. Another thing, she would ask me for something, and I would say "No" in a way that she couldn't take. Now I say "No" in a different way—easier and more matter of fact. Now I say "No" but then explain further. When I said "No," she would look at me as though I were destroying something in her.

T: Like you were killing something inside her, is that it?

F: Yes, yes. That's the way it was. (*Pause.*) I was going to drop this appointment, but I felt I had to come and face this.

T: You mean that something inside you made you come?

F: I have always had that feeling that I must face myself. Did Dee mention to you something about the time when she was close to me for several months and the relation was fine and cozy? One night she woke up crying, and from that time on, her actions became worse.

T: You feel that something happened that night to frighten her, is that it?

F: Dee and I talked it over, and we tried to think over what happened. Dee says I spoke in a sharp tone, but I really can't remember that I did.

T: You can't remember exactly what happened then.

F: Dee has often told me that I shouldn't make use of my voice in such a manner like—well, wanting perfection out of the child. That's one trouble about me. I don't want perfection, and yet when it isn't there, I want it. Whether it comes out of my back life or not, I'm not sure.

T: You mean there's something about you that insists on perfection and yet fights against it.

F: I will explain it the way I think. When I was twelve, I came to live with my real father and his second wife. My father had two children—my sister and me—in his former marriage and two children by this marriage, and she had one child by her former marriage. There were a lot of different personalities. It was obvious that I was the black sheep of the family. I was called a dumbbell practically every other day. My father never put his foot down.

T: I gather they made you feel very unimportant and very stupid.

F: You see, my brother Mike, who is now a dancer, was given lessons on the piano, and my sister, too, but they figured I was too dumb to take lessons. Yet I like music. I can sit down at the piano and can play by ear, and I have always loved it. I was never given a chance to go to college. When the crash came, I had to help out and give everything I earned home. Years later I felt very resentful at that. Down deep I have no hatred for anyone. Yet I know I don't love anyone from my family.

T: You mean in spite of what's happened, down deep you can't hate anyone.

F: I couldn't tolerate it within myself that I would really deeply hate anyone.

T: I gather you would consider that a weakness.

F: I don't know. I don't want to be hated. Since I have been married to Dee, I have known real love. When I lived with my parents, I never thought I would marry a girl who would consider me good enough to love her. I felt no woman would ever want me and say "I love you."

T: You mean you didn't feel good enough for that sort of affection.

F: Yes. I never brought friends up to the house. I never had the feeling that they would be wanted. This is something that's passing, and yet it all comes back. One time I was going to meet a girl. I thought she was good-looking. My stepmother saw her and made a remark about the girl not being good-looking at all, and that struck me that no good-looking girl would ever go with me. That's the way I took her remark. That's what I thought she meant. Now I can see her ignorance made her that way.

T: Now you feel you understand what made her say things like that.

F: I'm not stupid. I got over that. I did it when I ran away from home—when I met Dee and got married. With her I was a king, and that did more for me than anything. If someone hates me now, I don't care. I have got my wife and child and make a living, and I am a happy person.

T: As long as you have their love, then you can really feel happy.

F: The more friends I could have in the old days, the better I thought it was for me, and I had quite a few friends outside my home—people who really liked me. Actually, is it possible to be one thing inside the home and another outside? In my friends I found full expression, but I couldn't at home.

T: You feel, then, they helped you to be yourself.

F: I know it, because I wouldn't say it if it weren't true, but I was repressed at home. I was free outside. It was a very poor relation between me and my father and stepmother. My wife is the only person who ever made me feel wanted.

She loved me for what I was. Now she tells me she sees real goodness in me. Anything that I could do good in, I felt the fullest enjoyment from, and I felt good when someone outside told me I could do good. That's why sometimes I act childish when someone says I do well. I revel in it.

T: You really are affected by other people's praises.

F: That's how my wife looks at me. She respects me. It has been wonderful for me.

T: She has really helped you to gain faith in yourself.

F: (*Pause.*) It is just a few days, I have been thinking, that Kathy will get over her fears and she will come back to a normal relationship with me. Now I know it will take time. This fear of hers is great, but I know she can't have it all of her life.

T: You're pretty sure, then, that she'll get over it.

F: It isn't so important for me that she return to the deep affection. I want her to be normal. I don't want her to be different. If she's over the fears, then she can be herself.

T: In other words, you want her to get over the fears for her own sake, and you don't care so much whether the former deep relationship returns.

F: Maybe, maybe not. The only thing is I want her to be normal, but I can't say I want Kathy to be a normal child at any price.

T: I see.

F: I don't want to lose her affection, and yet I want her to lose her fears. I feel that if she returns to normalcy, then our former relationship will return. If she gets over the fears, then it will come back. It is just the idea of me being very patient with the child and facing the situation with kindness and love.

T: You mean you can look at her fears and her with more love than you have before.

F: Maybe that's right. (*Pause.*) If I sit down and go like this, Kathy will do the same thing. She wants to do everything I do. Just between you and me, Dee told me I shouldn't try to make Kathy be happy all the time, and I think it's just an excellent suggestion. Instead of saying, "Don't do that," to her in harsh tone, I could try to explain that I have something to do and that I will play with her later.

T: You mean you could accept her feelings about it and at the same time set a limit.

F: You brought up another point there. I once told Dee that I felt Kathy needs to be told something and that was final. In other words, there are some things that she just must learn to accept as part of living. Here's something—I don't do it any more, but a couple of times I used to say, "If you don't get in here by the time I count three, I will come and get you." Then one time she was fooling around in the sink way past her bedtime, and she said, "Aren't you going to count to three, Daddy?" She had that look in her eye, and it really made me feel bad, so I said, "Go ahead, honey. Finish what you're doing." Then I said, "I won't count any more." I didn't want her to reject me. I had the feeling that she wanted to be bossed or spanked. I felt she wanted to be spanked. I felt she wanted me to say, "You really can't do that," and that she wanted me to stick to it.

T: You mean she felt more secure when you set some limits.

F: That's another way of putting what I am trying to say. I see what you're trying to say. Now when we go up there at night, she decides she wants to clean the sink out. I figure this way lately: "Anyway, it wouldn't hurt."

T: In other words, as long as it doesn't hurt anybody, you might as well let her do it.

F: I have noticed Dee takes that viewpoint. I now have it clear in my mind. I am just going to be myself. I have been afraid before that she would reject me, but now I know I must do what I feel is right. I now realize I can make a decision and stand by it. This has helped a lot. I feel right. This is what I can do. I won't be back unless I get into a turmoil again, but I don't feel that I will.

NOVEMBER 22. PLAY SESSION WITH KATHY

C: (*Runs into room. Picks up a hand puppet and examines it.*) What is that?

M: It's a puppet.

C: A puppet?

M: Mm-hm.

C: What do you do to puppets? What do you do with them? (*Handles puppet.*) Mommy, look. It's just like on television.

M: Mm-hm.

C: (*Hands puppet to mother and picks up a rubber knife.*) What do you do with this? How do you cut?

M: You know how.

C: What do you do with the knifes?

M: You cut with them.

C: How you cut? (*Extends knife to mother.*) Here. Reach over. Here.

M: Are you too lazy to walk over here?

C: Here, reach. Let's see how you cut.

M: You show me how to cut.

C: (*Cuts at table with knife.*) See how you cut? That's how you cut this. Hold it nice and straight and you cut. You cut oranges.

T: Is that what you're cutting? Oranges?

C: I'm gonna cut this for you and Mommy. You eat this part. Here's some for you. Here, you take this, Mommy. (*Pretends to hand something first to T, then to mother. Still handles knife.*) See how you cut, Mom. You cut like this.

M: Mm-hm.

C: I don't want to put that dirty knife in my mouth.

M: That's not very dirty.

C: (*Throws knife on the floor.*) Get this little shovel and dig in the dirt. There's a whole bunch of dirt. This goes in the yellow truck. (*Puts a spoonful of sand from sandbox into truck. Handles sand.*) A duty. I gotta make, Mommy.

M: All right.

C: (*Goes out to bathroom with mother. Walks back into room and picks up the steam shovel.*) Here's a steam shovel. Mommy's gonna get this. (*Hands a puppet to T.*) And here's a bunny for you. You can have that. (*Continues to play in sand.*)

* * * * *

C: (*Picks up gun and handles it. Aims at mother.*) Bang, bang, bang. (*Moves to sandbox and looks at T.*) I burned myself on popcorn. Where did you burn yourself, Mommy?

M: On the oven.

C: She burned herself on the oven.

T: And you hurt yourself on the popcorn popper.

C: Yes, I burned myself on the popcorn popper. I love popcorn. (*Dances around a little near the sandbox.*) You know, I don't like my Aunty Ann.

T: You don't?

C: No. What don't I like where my Aunty Ann lives?

M: Oh, you mean the sign?

C: Yes, the sign.

T: Is that why you don't like Aunty Ann? Because she has a sign near her house?

C: She lives by it, but she doesn't live way far from it.

T: Mm-hm.

C: (*Digs in the sandbox with the steam shovel. Carries some sand to truck.*) You're the stupid mother that I ever saw in my life.

M: You think I'm stupid, honey?

C: You're the most stupid old mother that I ever saw in my life. You're the stupid old mother that I ever saw.

T: She's the stupidest old mother you've ever seen, hm?

C: (*Handles steam shovel.*) Why is this dirty?

M: Well, you were using it in the sand.

C: Take this off.

M: You can take it off.

T: You want Mommy to do it, but she tells you to do it yourself, hm?

C: I want her to do it.

T: You want her to do it but she wants you to do it.

C: I always like to make her work. (*Brushes sand from hands while walking around room. Picks up small nursing bottle.*) Where's the baby?

T: Where could the baby be?

C: Where is she? Oh. (*Picks up small doll.*) I'm gonna wash the diaper in the washing machine so the diaper will be nice and clean. I want to soak it in the bottle. (*Picks up large nursing bottle.*) I need the big bottle. And I'll soak it right in the big bottle. Take the pin off. (*Watches T as he unpins doll's diaper. Takes the diaper off and lets the doll fall to the floor.*) Drop goes the baby.

T: She dropped right down on the floor, didn't she?

C: Soak. (*Dips doll's diaper into large bottle of water.*)

T: You want to stick it right down in there.

C: (*Continues to stuff diaper into bottle.*) Mommy, you hold this. You hold it. I'm tired of holding it.

M: You're tired?

C: (*Soaks diaper in bottle while mother holds the bottle.*)

T: You're poking it right down in there.

C: Oh! What you call it when I couldn't go on the merry-go-round? Polio?

M: Mm-hm.

C: Polio. Polio's a very bad cold. Polio's a *very* bad cold! Isn't polio a very bad cold?

M: Mm-hm.

C: Polio.

T: It's kind of a funny name, isn't it?

C: (*Still soaking diaper in bottle.*) Once when I took my boots off, my hands got all full of dirt.

T: You got your hands pretty dirty, hm?

C: Uh-huh. Then once I got my hands all full of mud.

T: You didn't like that, did you?

C: No. (*Removes diaper from bottle and squeezes water from it on the floor. Dips it into bottle again.*) And now I'll let it soak.

T: You're soaking it real good.

C: Now I'll take it. (*Takes bottle from mother and places it on table. Takes diaper out of bottle. Stamps on the floor.*) Voulez vous, Mom. Voulez vous. That's what Daddy says.

M: In French?

C: Yeah. In French. What does he say in French? (*Jumps up and down while holding diaper.*)

M: Voulez vous.

C: Voulez vous.

T: You like to talk about your daddy's French, hm?

C: When Daddy takes off his shoes and socks, he goes like this. Like this. Like that. (*Shows T how her father acts without shoes on.*)

M: Is that how Daddy keeps his feet when he hasn't got any shoes on?

C: Uh-huh.

T: You like to do what your daddy does?

C: When he hasn't got his shoes on, then he goes like this.

T: Is that what you like to do?

C: Uh-huh. When my feet are cold.

T: You like to be just like your daddy, hm?

C: (*Soaks diaper again.*) Stuck that in and let it soak. (*Drops sand into bottle.*) This has gotta go in dirty water.

T: Mm-hm.

C: (*Drops bells into bottle.*) It goes right in the water. Put your jingle in.

T: You'll put those in, too.

C: I'll put another jingle in. Those two jingles make that dry. It'll make that clean. (*Empties sand from truck into bottle. Sings "Yankee Doodle." Brushes sand off hands and looks at mother.*) I've gotta make a duty.

M: All right. Come on.

C: (*Walks out to bathroom with mother. Walks back into room and smiles at T.*) I drowned myself. I drowned myself.

T: You drowned yourself, hm?

C: (*Picks up doll and pushes its head into dish of water.*) Gonna stick her head in.

T: You're going to put her right into the water.

C: She has to make. She has to make sissy. (*Picks up a rubber cord and pushes it at doll's genital area.*) She has to make. O.K., come on. Make sissy. Come on, make duty. Now you have to make. (*Pushes cord in water on floor. Picks up dish and spills water on floor near puppet. Places dish and doll on chair and sticks cord into large nursing bottle.*) Take the diaper out. It smells. It's gonna be all smelly. (*Hands bottle with diaper in it to mother.*) Here's the diaper. Will you get the diaper out? Will you get the diaper out?

T: You really want Mommy to get the diaper out, hm?

C: Get the diaper out. (*Takes bottle back from mother and tries to shake the diaper out of it.*) Here it is. Now.

T: Well, Kathy, that's all the time we have left today. Our time is just up.

C: Mommy, will you read me a magazine? (*Looks at T.*) Bye.

T: Good-by, Kathy.

C: Bye. (*Walks out of room with mother.*)

Discussion: November 22 Play Session

Kathy continues the repeated questions to her mother, showing that she is still generally anxious in the play therapy situation. Her hostility toward her mother becomes direct. She picks up a toy gun, aims it at her mother, and shouts, "Bang, bang, bang." Then she expresses feelings of anger against an aunt. Later she looks at her mother and says, "You're the stupidest mother that I ever saw in my life . . . You're the most stupid old mother that I ever saw." Kathy asks her mother to remove sand from a shovel and explains, "I always like to make her work."

The diaper-washing play begins again. Her cleanliness anxiety is further explored as she scrubs the diaper and indicates to the therapist that she does not like to see dirt on herself.

Kathy shows her positive identification with her father in the playroom, repeating what he says and mimicking his behavior.

Toward the end of the session the compulsive behavior reappears. Kathy picks up the baby doll and shouts, "She has to make. She has to make sissy. She has to make. O.K., come on. Make sissy. Come on, make duty. Now you have to make." This episode may reflect the pressures Kathy has faced in the toileting demands at home.

NOVEMBER 22. TELEPHONE CONVERSATION WITH FATHER

F: I wanted to talk to you. Before I came to see you, my stomach would turn over. I couldn't eat and I couldn't sleep. I didn't know how to act. I would be afraid to do anything for fear it would be the wrong thing. All I thought about was that. Now I've been eating and sleeping more regularly. I've been working without being worried.

I talked to my wife about what you told me. Will you explain to her in your own way? That was the whole key as far as discipline is concerned. I hardly ever gave her any discipline at all, yet she seemed like she wanted to be told she couldn't do certain things. I tried to explain it to Dee but found it difficult. I understood it in terms of myself, but it was difficult to explain it to her so she could see it in terms of herself.

When it was time to eat, Kathy would pick up one plate and another and another. She was never satisfied. A couple of nights ago I said, "Kathy, you will eat from that plate. You don't have to eat if you don't want to." Two seconds later she ate the whole plate and talked and laughed throughout the whole meal. She seemed perfectly satisfied. And furthermore, I think that no matter how I treated her she would always love me anyway. No matter how much discipline I used, within limits, she would always love me and I would love her.

One more point I noticed. You have made me see things I haven't seen. I may have been too mixed up. Now I am not. Sometimes I've noticed during the day we're right in the room and she'll say, "Where are you?" I realized if I don't answer she goes right on in her play. I am not afraid any more. I feel good now. I don't worry about her at work. Now I am like I was before. I haven't changed myself. I am still myself. I'm happy about things now. Well, I won't take any more of your time. Thank you very much.

November 23. Interview with Mother

M: I don't know what happened, but she's just as changed as ever. After the last time I talked to you we let her sleep on the daybed, and then we ordered a Hollywood bed. That part has settled the sleeping problem, but something might still crop up.

Today she wanted to play with her finger paints, and I

said, "We have to go downtown first," and she said, "O.K.,"
right away, whereas before when she wanted to do something, she was determined to do it right at that moment.

There is something I wanted to tell you that I forgot.
Remember when I told you she didn't want to have anything to do with her daddy? She was just clinging to me. I
know she loves me, and it doesn't bother me. In order to
get her to make up to him, I kept saying, "Go to Daddy."

I kept saying "Go to Daddy," and the way I said it may
have made her feel I didn't want her. I have shown her in
every way I could that I love her.

T: You mean she may have felt you didn't want her, even though
you have shown her that you loved her.

M: Maybe she felt that I rejected her, too, because she wouldn't
go to Daddy and then, see, I would say, "Let Daddy dress
you." I was trying to get her out of it by pushing her. When
she was mad at her father, I think she should have been
allowed to get it out of her system.

T: You feel she should have been allowed to bring out her feelings, no matter how they affected your husband.

M: Yes. Something else I wanted to ask you. I don't know how
to act when I am in the playroom. I try to act the way you
do. I am a little strained. I felt silly. If I see she's having
difficulty, then I help her. If I am myself, it won't change
anything. She doesn't talk about it. She says, "Are we going to see Mr. C? Are we going to play today?"

T: She looks forward to coming here then.

M: Let's see if there was something else. She's not afraid of any
signs any more. She'll say, "I don't like the arm." Today I
went right by it and explained to her, and she stared right
at it, and she said, "Oh, look there, Mommy. You went
right by that sign," and she laughed about it. She had no
connection with her fears. I have not noticed any fears at
all. She's not as rebellious as she was. She doesn't like to go
to bed yet, but it's not because she's afraid. She just likes
to stay up with us. We got hold of you right away when
the fears first started. They had only gone for a short time.
I hope it is disappearing forever now.

After she'd leave the playroom, sometimes for the next few days she'd go on playing like she played there. I can't understand how these fears first came about. I see mothers beating their kids and so on, and they don't have any difficulty. She's very seldom reprimanded.

Would you say this is all right? She has a lot of blue jeans, and she'd get everything dirty, and when I saw her clothes running out, I'd have to wash them all again. I decided she's got the slacks and blue jeans, and I said, "Now look, Kathy." I told her, "You're going to wear such and such in the mornings and that's all there is to it. In the afternoon you can wear a dress if you want." I said this after talking with my husband.

T: You just decided that you'd have to set a limit there.

M: Yes, and I started insisting she wear either her slacks or skirts in the morning. The first time she kind of pouted, but now she doesn't even question it.

What about these adenoids? Do you think it's all right for her to have them taken out at this time?

T: Whatever decision you and Kathy's doctor can come to will be the most satisfactory one.

M: He told me when she was about three that she ought to have them out. The last four days her adenoids have not been bad. She has a horror of doctors.

By the way, she made me take the books in the car today. She wanted them. She'd always say, "Hide the books —take them away," before. Today they're in the car, and she took them with her. I took out one book, and there was a puppy in it. I said, "We have only three books, and you don't have to look at the puppy." Before she was so terrified you couldn't do anything with her, but now, as you help her, she not only listened to the story but later asked to see the puppy.

T: You mean there are ways of making her feel more relaxed at these times.

M: That's what I mean. She couldn't stand it before. I feel very much better about the whole thing, because she is improving. You wouldn't ever know what we went through.

She used to be terrified. There are no more eyes now, no more fear of eyes.

I meant to tell you—when she plays in the yard she'll sit down and sit at the sand and play for a long time like she would in the playroom. This has all started recently. She does that all the time. Not seeing those books for three months, she read, the other day she read by heart every one of them that she has, so she must have a pretty good memory to be able to do that.

(*Pause.*) I guess there won't be any need for me to come down any more, but if you decide that there are other things that come up later, in terms of Kathy's play in the playroom, then I'll make an appointment with you.

DECEMBER 5. PLAY SESSION WITH KATHY

C: (*Runs into the room. Walks near T and then goes to pile of furniture.*) Where's the diaper?

T: I wonder where that is.

C: (*Touches larger doll on bench.*) Take the diaper off this baby. Mommy! (*Runs out to hall to find mother.*)

M: I'm coming in.

T: You like to have Mommy right near you.

C: Here. Here's a mask.

T: You want me to have a mask. O.K.

C: No. Mommy wear a mask. (*Takes mask from T and gives it to mother.*) I'm gonna make supper. (*Sits near table. Stands up to move chair closer, then sits down again. Picks up dish and walks to mother.*) Well, I don't need the chopping bowl. Gonna make chopped liver. I—Mommy—Mommy, do you make chopped liver? I like chopped liver.

M: Mm-hm.

C: (*Picks up sieve, fills it with sand, then empties it into dish.*) Gonna have chopped liver. You can make it a different kind. See this, Mommy? That's to make chopped liver with. Pick it up and put it in here.

T: You pick it up and you throw it in. That's how.

C: Now there's no more liver. Now I'm gonna chop it. (*Holds dish with sand in lap and chops at sand with shovel.*) This is a neat chopping bowl. Baby's gonna have some of that, too. I gotta chop it.

T: You want the baby to have the chopped liver, hm?

C: Oh! There we go. (*Spills some sand on her socks.*) On my sock. I did it on purpose.

T: You mean you put it on you on purpose, hm?

C: These are my good socks. I wear them every day.

T: And you didn't care. You did it anyway.

C: Here we go again. (*Spills sand on her dress and brushes it off. Stirs sand with shovel.*) Daddy says, "I don't love you."

T: Daddy says that he doesn't love you, hm?

C: No. I say I don't love Daddy.

T: Oh, you don't love Daddy.

C: No. Daddy said if I don't eat dinner, then he doesn't bring me any surprises. He says, "If you won't eat, then I won't bring you any surprises."

T: Oh, your daddy tells you you've got to eat, hm?

C: Uh-huh.

T: And you don't like that, is that it?

C: I'll play with chopped liver. Once Donna threw sand once. In my eyes once.

T: She threw sand right in your eyes.

C: And Mommy had to wash it out. (*Starts to chop sand with shovel again.*) It's dirty over here. Do you know that, Mommy?

T: You don't like the dirt, hm?

C: No. Just the sand. I don't like how soft and sticky it gets. It always makes me sad.

T: That makes you sad, hm?

C: Uh-huh. It's always hard to make. You chop and you chop and you go like this. (*Straightens her skirt out. Looks for her slip.*) You forgot the slip, Mommy!

M: You've got a slip on.

C: Where? I see.

T: Almost thought you didn't have a slip on, hm?

C: But I did. In case I be cold. (*Picks up puppet and shows it to mother.*) Is it a mask?

M: Does it look like a mask?

C: Does he talk?

M: What do you think? Does he talk?

C: No, he can't. (*Drops puppet on the floor and sits on chair again.*)

T: There. Down he goes.

C: I don't like him.

T: You don't like him, hm?

C: No. I don't like him 'cause he's a puppet.

M: You don't like the puppets?

C: No. (*Continues to chop sand in dish.*) And I'll chop, chop, chop. Chopping, chopping, chop, chop, chop. Gonna make it. It's gonna be ready in just a couple minutes. Mommy's gonna have good chopped liver. (*Puts dish on table and brushes sand from her hands. Picks up rubber doll and feeds it with small bottle.*) The baby has to drink water 'cause she's thirsty. She'll have to stay right here. Like this she can drink.

T: Mm-hm.

C: She's gotta drink a lot of water. She doesn't drink the water.

T: She doesn't?

C: Gonna drink all the water up. Chopped liver is ready, baby. (*Puts bottle on table and feeds doll sand from dish with spoon.*)

T: It's all ready for the baby.

C: Uh-huh. She likes chopped liver. If I make chopped liver for her, she always eats it up. She always likes it. She always likes chopped liver.

T: She really likes to eat that.

C: Mm-hm. (*Continues to spoon sand into the doll's mouth.*) She's got a surprise coming. You know what it is? A sucker.

T: That will be a real surprise.

C: I know. She's getting a sucker and chocolate. And bubble gum.

T: Three surprises, and all for her.

C: Mm-hm.

T: She must like surprises.

C: She does. I never get that many surprises.

T: You never get that many surprises, hm?

C: No. She likes that chopped liver. Eat, baby. Eat, baby. Eat, baby. She says she likes chopped liver.

T: That's what she says.

C: She doesn't waste it. She keeps it all in her mouth. Eat, baby. Eat, baby.

T: You tell the baby to eat and the baby eats.

C: Eat, baby. She says, "Yes, I will eat."

T: She eats when you tell her to.

C: (*Feeds doll with small bottle.*) Swallow, baby. Good. She likes—she can't swallow it.

T: No?

C: No, she can't. Oh, good thing she doesn't like chopped liver.

M: Why?

C: 'Cause she doesn't.

T: She just decided that she didn't like it.

C: (*Feeds doll more sand.*) Also, she can't have no more surprises. (*Stamps her foot on the floor.*)

T: No more surprises for her, hm?

C: No.

T: Because she won't eat her chopped liver.

C: No. She doesn't like it.

T: She must feel bad.

C: But she's gonna eat a little bit. (*Feeds doll a small spoonful of sand.*)

T: Oh, now she's going to eat some.

C: Come on, baby. Take a little bit. You always have to eat it all. She's gotta eat that or no chocolate.

T: She's got to have that or nothing else.

C: (*Leaves doll on the table. Picks up a sheet of paper and cuts it into small pieces. Dips piece of paper into large bottle of water and then places wet paper on car.*) Put that on the back of the car. There. Now. (*Wets more pieces of paper.*) Now. Put some right on this truck. (*Pastes wet pieces of paper on cars and trucks for the remainder of the hour.*)

Discussion: December 5 Play Session

For the first time, up to this point, Kathy spills sand on herself and is not at all perturbed. She gets sand on her good socks and does not care about it. Kathy says she does not love her daddy and explains, "Daddy said if I don't eat dinner, then he doesn't bring me any surprises." The implication or connection in Kathy's mind seems to be, "If I don't eat, Daddy won't love me." Kathy has frequently shown, in her play, strong feelings and associations against forced feedings. Feeding the doll figures begins again, but now the feelings are more positive. The baby is not "forced" to eat. "She always likes chopped liver," says Kathy. The baby really likes to eat. Kathy reenacts the feeding scene over and over again in this session. She shows some ambivalence at points. The baby likes to eat and she does not like to eat. The baby is warned a number of times that unless she eats, there will be no surprises and no chocolate. Kathy releases a great deal of feeling as she explores and reexplores these negative and ambivalent attitudes.

December 5. Telephone Conversation with Father

10 A.M.

F: I just got an idea that may be the cause of it all. Probably not, but Dee thinks so. She thinks that Kathy has a fear that we will leave her. If we go on the street, she's afraid we're going to send her away. She thinks we'll leave her and she won't see us again. Now we're worried, though not as much as before. She talks more about her fears. Will she outgrow this? If you were to say "yes" and mean it, then I would never have any worries.

Last night she started to whimper. I said, "There's no reason to cry. I'm here, and I'll protect you. You don't have to cry," and she stopped crying. We've been losing sleep. She'd wake up and cry and whimper, but this time when we went in, she told us what she was afraid of. Personally, I don't care. We'll just have to string along until she gets better. Kathy is no different from other children. All children have fears. She'll get over this.

3 P.M.

F: Last Monday night Kathy woke up and was terrified and saw a shadow on the wall. She has awakened many nights in the last two weeks just like she used to when she was upset. Tuesday afternoon she saw puppets, and then she said she saw the same puppets in your school. Tuesday evening she came running and said somebody was trying to catch her but she ran away. There was a light shining in the window. She turned away and asked me to get rid of it. A little later she went into the kitchen. She ran and said a mosquito was running after her. She said she was afraid of a man in the furnace. A couple of nights ago I put her to bed. We had been taking turns. After she was in bed she said, "I want Mommy to put me to bed," and then she said it over and over and over. I said, "Mommy doesn't have to put you in bed." Finally she fell asleep.

It's sensible for her to understand that when she's in bed, she might want Dee near her. I haven't changed any. I'm shaking just a little because it's really bothering me. It was going beautifully. If she woke up at night, just a few words and she went back to sleep. And now a lot of it has started again. I myself can see where it will pass in due time, but it comes back to what is it? I can't find out. I don't know what's in back of it. What the symbol is I don't know. I'm not worried about it actually. I was afraid her mind would go blank. Now I feel that I wish it would pass. I have to go back to work now. (*Pause.*)

She can't make up her mind. She'll just keep changing. First she'll want one thing and then another. She'll say, "I don't want this. I do want this. I don't want this."

T: I gather it's pretty irritating to you.

F: She's very, very indefinite. Sometimes she says, "I want Mommy to put me to bed," and she won't hear anything I say to her. She just seems to go deaf. You just have to yell to pierce the wall of her thinking. Before I put her to bed she'd say, "I want Mommy to put me to bed." Finally she'd agree to let me put her to bed. I tell her, "Mommy isn't going to put

you to bed. She's got other things to do. I'm going to put you
to bed, or else you can go to bed by yourself."

I guess that's all. I'm glad you let me talk to you.

DECEMBER 13. PLAY SESSION WITH KATHY

C: (*Runs into the room.*)

T: Well, everything is all set for you, Kathy.

C: O.K. (*Carries chair to table and sits down.*) Mommy.

M: Hmm?

C: Mommy, my feet are frozen.

M: Well, they'll warm up.

C: This is a little balloon. Here. That little balloon for you. (*Hands
T a small balloon.*) And a big balloon for Mommy. Here's a
big one for you.

M: Thank you.

C: And you've got a little balloon. (*Picks up puppets from floor
and hands them to T.*) Here's a puppet for you. Two puppets.

T: You want me to have those, hm?

C: There's a toad chasing me, Mom. (*Runs to mother and hugs
her. Looks at T.*)

T: A toad is chasing you?

C: Yes.

T: Are you afraid he's going to get you?

C: Yeah.

T: That's what you're afraid of, hm?

C: There's a bad toad catching me, Mom.

T: You really are afraid of that toad.

C: You're gonna get a puppet. A different kind of puppet. Here's
your puppet. A pretty puppet. Here's another puppet. You
got two puppets, too. (*Hands two animal puppets to
mother.*)

M: Thank you.

C: (*Picks up large nursing bottle.*) I don't drink water out of this.

T: You don't?

C: No. Babies drink out of that. I don't have to wash the diapers
every time.

T: You don't have to wash them every time?

C: No. (*Holds doll and sits on chair.*) Every time she wears them, every time they get dirty. (*Dips rubber cord into bottle and pushes cord into doll's mouth.*) You like water? She says "I like water very much." That's what she likes. She says "I want some water."

T: And you let her have the water.

C: No surprises for her.

T: You didn't give her any surprises, hm?

C: No. Because she didn't like water. She wants some milk now.

T: Is that what she wants?

C: Yes. She wants some milk. (*Pause.*) Daddy teases me.

T: He really teases you. And do you like that?

C: Well, yes, I like that. When I chew the gum he laughs at me.

T: He laughs at you then.

C: Mm-hm. (*Picks up small bottle.*) Baby, baby. Wash your hair. You need a shampoo. (*Wants mother to remove the nipple from bottle.*) Get this off. I gotta wash her hair.

M: You can do it yourself.

C: I can't.

M: Try it.

C: No. (*Mother removes nipple and C empties water from small bottle into dish. Empties water from dish into sandbox. Puts sand in dish with steam shovel.*) I'll wash your hair.

T: You'll wash her hair?

C: Yes. (*Crouches by sandbox.*) I'm getting dirty today. (*Pause.*) Mommy has skim milk, but I don't like skim milk. Mommy's on a diet. I'm not on a diet. (*Mother laughs.*)

T: Oh.

C: (*Fills dish with sand and carries it to table. Picks up doll and holds it over dish.*) She has to make sissy. She has to make sissy. (*Wants T to unpin doll's diaper.*) Unpin it. Unpin it.

T: There we are.

C: (*Holds diaperless doll over dish.*) Make. She doesn't have to.

T: She doesn't have to make sissy?

C: (*Hands diaper to mother.*) Here. You're gonna hold the diaper.

M: O.K.

C: (*Picks up some sand and rubs it all over doll's head.*) I'll just wash this right off. (*Stands up and brushes sand from dress vigorously.*) My good dress!

T: It's all sandy and you don't like that.

C: No. It's the best dress I ever bought.

T: Oh.

C: My hands are dirty. (*Picks up rubber knife. Pokes at sand in hand with knife.*) This is a big knife. It's sharp. It's sharp. You know that, Mom?

M: Mm-hm.

C: (*Pokes blade of knife on palm of her hand.*) This knife is really sharp. Sharp, sharp, sharp. (*Puts knife back on table and picks up shovel. Chops at sand in dish.*) Chop, chop. (*Continues to chop at sand.*) Baby, your chopped liver is ready. Do you like chopped liver? What do you want to eat it with? This? No, you gotta eat it out of this.

T: She has to eat it out of what you tell her to.

C: A spoon. (*Feeds doll sand from spoon.*) If she wants some chopped liver, she says, "I want some chopped liver." And I made it for her. Just for her.

T: No one else can have any.

C: No. Eat it. She's trying to get it all in her mouth but she can't. (*Settles herself in chair and holds dish and doll. Sighs.*) Well.

T: She tries and tries but she can't do it.

C: (*Looks at mother, then at T.*) You remember when Donna used to throw sand in my eyes? And I used to throw sand back in her eyes.

T: She used to do that, hm?

C: Yeah. And I used to throw sand in her eyes. And I didn't like that, and Mommy had to wash the sand out.

T: Mm-hm.

C: Poor baby. She's thirsty. Well, baby, you're gonna get something. Oh, she likes it. (*Puts doll on table and picks up dish with sand. Walks to mother.*) Now, Mommy. Hold my gum. (*Gives mother her chewing gum.*)

M: O.K., dear.

C: (*Looks at T.*) Can you put it in your mouth, like that?

T: Do you suppose I could?

C: How you put it in your mouth?

T: You show me.

C: O.K. Like this. (*Puts some sand on paddle and tastes it. Spits sand out on floor.*)

T: It doesn't taste too good, does it?

C: I don't like it. (*Stirs paddle around in dish. Tastes sand again and makes a face.*) You know, sand is sour. Is sand sour?

T: What do you think?

C: It's not sour but it tastes sour to me. (*Tastes more sand and spits it back into dish.*) It's not sour but it tastes sour. (*Wipes mouth with diaper.*) The diaper's dirty anyway. It's like a towel. (*Tastes more sand and spits it out.*)

T: You don't like to keep that in your mouth, hm?

C: But I like it.

T: You really like it.

C: (*Eats and spits sand again.*) Pooh! That's what I used to say when I had sand in my house.

T: You used to say pooh?

C: Uh-huh. I like this sand. (*Leans against mother and digs in sand with paddle.*)

M: Honey, do you want your gum?

C: (*Dances up and down in front of mother.*) I don't want it. I don't want to chew it. Throw it away! Throw the gum away. In the street. Throw it away in the street! (*Puts dish on table and picks up a balloon. Runs back and forth across room.*) I can run fast.

T: You can?

C: Mm-hm. Let me show you. Let me show you how fast. Let me show you. (*Runs across room.*) I can run real fast. Here comes a wolf! (*Runs to mother and waves balloon in the air.*)

T: You can run real fast when the wolf is coming, can't you?

C: Yes. Right against the wall.

T: You really hit the wolf, hm?

C: Yes. He wants to take the balloon away.

T: Does he want to take it away?

C: No. He wants to throw it away in the street. (*Jumps up and down, and balloon falls into sandbox. Picks it up and leans against mother.*) There's a wolf!

T: You're really afraid of the wolf, hm?

C: Yes. I am. (*Waves balloon around.*) I'm afraid of the toads.

T: You're afraid of the toads?

C: Mm-hm. (*Tosses balloon aside and picks up bells. Jingles them and jumps up and down. Places bells on chair and turns to mother.*) I wanta go now. Now.

T: You want to leave now, Kathy?

C: Yes.

T: You still have a minute or so left if you want to stay. You can go if you want to, though. It's up to you.

C: I wanta stay.

T: You want to stay for two more minutes?

C: Uh-huh. (*Picks up bells again.*)

T: O.K.

C: And now, where's a knife? Where's a knife? I can't find the knife.

T: You need the knife, hm?

C: The knife. Here's a knife, but I don't want to use that knife. (*Picks up a rubber knife but puts it back on table.*) Everything I pick up, I put down. (*Holds balls and runs to mother.*) Here comes the wolf! The bad wolf! Let me sit in your lap.

T: The real bad wolf is coming and you're afraid.

C: Yes. Let me sit in your lap. (*Settles herself in mother's lap.*) Now. Now he can't hurt me.

T: You mean when you're on Mommy's lap, the wolf can't hurt you?

C: No, he can't hurt me. (*Sits in mother's lap and jingles the bells.*)

T: Kathy, our time is up for today.

C: (*Hands T the bells and helps mother put down the toys she has been holding.*) I'll be back. (*Walks out of the room with mother and T.*)

Discussion: December 13 Play Session

Kathy enacts in the playroom the fears she has shown outside. She runs to her mother, claiming that "the bad toad" is after her. She stays near her mother for awhile, then starts playing again. She shows positive feelings toward her father again, imitating his behavior with enjoyment. She indicates further growth in her attitude about cleanliness, exclaiming, "I'm getting dirty today."

Kathy plays out the forced toileting scene but uses less pressure on the "baby" this time. She plays more freely in the sand for a long time. Suddenly her fears return, and she runs to her mother, claiming that a wolf is chasing her. Then, showing she is not so frightened any more, she strikes back at the imaginary wolf. Near the end of the session she becomes frightened again and sits on her mother's lap.

December 14. Interview with Mother

M: I'll tell you what I learned. She said there was a wolf chasing her, trying to chase her out of the house. She would get hurt by a car and would go far, far away and wouldn't see Mommy and Daddy again. Or else she would get burned by a fire. Maybe we stressed that harm might come to her too much, if she wasn't careful. She keeps asking questions. Maybe she's afraid.

She used to wake up and cry. Now that we've tried to understand her feelings, she wakes up and tells us about her fears. She talks to us. She tells us. She used to draw away from my husband, but now she doesn't. She'll hold onto either one of us.

I belong to a club, and they had a psychologist. I listened to him, and he said most adults handle children like little adults instead of trying to handle a child. I went to a meeting, and that's what a psychologist said.

She saw a toad on Howdy Doody, and she said this toad was trying to chase her out of the house. All of a sudden she has started this clinging business. The wolf I know she got from her books. I remember once I said to her, "Kathy, if you don't behave, I'll call it off." She misunderstood and said, "Why are you going to call the wolf?" I think I have it all figured out, and then when I think about it, I get all mixed up. She talks about the wolf trying to chase her. She lay there in bed until nine-thirty. This goes on every night. She thinks and thinks and thinks before she goes to bed. Every car that goes by reflects on the wall. In her room, the same thing happens.

I would like to know what brought it back in the first place. She was just fine. She used to sing in bed. Now she wakes up continually. For four nights I had to sleep with her, but she never slept. She couldn't have slept more than five hours a night. We tried to give her confidence. We're befuddled. When she's well rested when she gets up she's better. She doesn't think too much, so she doesn't think of the fears. She's still afraid of the strong arm. My husband would say, "Honey, don't be afraid of anything. We won't let anything hurt you." He'd say, "You see this arm, honey? I can protect you with it." He'd show her it, and now she's afraid of that arm. At home he goes around wearing polo shirts, and he'd show her his strong arm. It seems to be the logical connection.

T: You feel she's afraid of him, then.

M: Of course she's afraid of other things. She doesn't like the giraffe on the sign. Yesterday she said the bad eye was chasing her. Remember the bird on the telephone book? She said that the bird is in the room. What made her all right during that period? What made her go back? Before, we tried to reason with her. Now when she's afraid of something, I try to understand it. When she told me about the car hurting her and our going away, I said, "If you get hurt by a car or if you get burned or get hurt, we'll always be there." I tried to show her we'd be there with her.

I know she loves her daddy. When he comes home, she's so excited she can hardly wait for him to come home. She's that way about him.

December 20. Play Session with Kathy

C: (*Hands T two puppets.*) Here. You're gonna have those two puppets.

T: You want me to have these two, hm?

C: Mommy's gonna get the other puppets. Here, Mommy. (*Hands mother animal puppets.*)

T: Mommy gets those two and I get these two.

C: Yeah. Don't you mind getting those two puppets, Mommy?

M: No, honey. I don't mind.

C: (*Walks back and forth across room.*) You know what? I got something to tell you. You know what the flub-a-dub wanted?

T: What did the flub-a-dub want?

C: He says, "I want a present." The flub-a-dub says, "I want some spaghetti and meatballs." (*Jumps up and down and laughs.*) That's so funny.

T: You like to tell such funny things, don't you?

C: Yeah. (*Laughs again.*) Isn't that funny? (*Picks up a boat and crouches by sandbox. Fills boat with sand.*) Now I'm gonna make some sand. I'm gonna smooth the sand out. (*Hands boat to mother.*) Here, Mom. Here's some for you. You're gonna get this. With a little shovel. Here, eat it. (*Walks around room.*) A wolf's chasing me!

T: Is a wolf chasing you, Kathy?

C: A wolf's catching me.

T: Oh, catching you. The big bad wolf. And are you afraid?

C: No. I'm not afraid. I'm not afraid of the wolf. (*Picks up a paddle from the table.*) This is what I was looking for.

T: So that's what you were looking for.

C: Uh-huh.

T: And now you found it.

C: (*Tastes some sand from boat with paddle.*) I'm eating my supper. I'm gonna eat my supper now. (*Sits down on chair and tastes more sand.*) I'm gonna give Daddy dinner.

T: You're giving Daddy his dinner?

C: Yes. He's gonna eat out of the shovel. And I'll eat out of it.

T: You and Daddy will eat out of the same shovel.

C: No, he's gonna eat the shovel.

T: Oh, he's going to eat the shovel?

C: Mm-hm. Where's the shovel? No shovels. So Daddy will have to go to bed. (*Tastes sand and makes a face.*) He'll have to go to bed with no surprises.

T: No surprise for Daddy, hm?

C: No. 'Cause he wasn't good.

T: He wasn't good to you, hm?

C: No.

T: So to bed with him without anything.

C: Yeah. And he didn't want to go to bed.

T: He didn't?

C: No.

T: He didn't like not having surprises, hm?

C: No. He doesn't like not having surprises. (*Handles paddle and tastes sand. Looks at T.*) I forgot to give Daddy a drink of water, and he was thirsty.

T: He was thirsty, and you forgot to give Daddy a drink of water, hm?

C: But I'm not gonna.

T: You're not going to do it?

C: No. (*Eats some more sand.*)

T: He'll have to go without any.

C: Uh-huh. I didn't kiss him good night.

T: Didn't you?

C: Uh-huh. (*Takes puppets from mother, together with two on floor, and hands them to T.*) And you're gonna get puppets. Here's puppets for you.

T: All the puppets are going to me.

C: 'Cause Mommy doesn't want any puppets.

T: She doesn't, hm?

C: (*Looks at mother.*) She has to stay up. And a surprise for Mommy.

T: Oh, you're going to give Mommy a surprise, are you?

C: Mm-hm. (*Tastes more sand and spits it out on the floor.*) Then a drink of water, and then she's going upstairs to bed.

T: Oh, I see. You'll do that for Mommy, hm?

C: Mmmm. And tonight is my dinner, and I'm going right up. And no surprise.

T: No surprise for you either.

C: No, 'cause I don't want surprises.

T: You don't even like them.

C: Daddy always brings me surprises.

T: He does?

C: Mmmm.

T: And are you happy about that?

C: (*Sighs heavily. Tastes sand again, then spits it on the floor.*) Pooh!

T: It doesn't taste so good.

C: (*Stamps foot on the floor.*) Stamp, stamp. (*Hands mother the rubber cord.*) That silly old thing! This silly old thing that I ever saw! (*Hands mother the large doll.*) Mommy's gonna get all the presents.

T: They're all for Mommy.

C: And you're gonna get—here's a present for you. (*Hands T a small doll figure.*) You're gonna get all the presents. (*Hands T another small male doll.*) And Mommy's gonna get a girl. (*Hands mother a female doll.*)

M: Thank you, honey.

C: You're gonna get all the presents. Some more presents. You're gonna get all of 'em. (*Gives mother another small doll.*) Here's another present. (*Picks up dish and moves to sandbox. Fills dish with sand.*) Now I'll fix some chopped liver.

T: Chopped liver, hm?

C: Yeah.

T: You just feel like chopping some liver.

C: Mm-hm. And get another bunch of chopped liver. (*Chops sand in dish with paddle.*)

T: More chopped liver to chop, chop, chop.

C: (*Fills dish with more sand.*) Now get some more. And have another big bite. And still another big bite.

T: It goes on and on and on.

C: Yeah. It goes on and on and on. Gonna chop. (*Stamps foot on floor a few times.*) Stinky! Stinky! Stinky! (*Picks up doll. Sits on chair and pushes some sand into doll's mouth.*) What do you want? A drink of water? Here we go again! (*Re-places doll on table and walks back and forth across room.*)

T: All she asks for is more water and causes a lot of trouble.

C: Yeah. And she doesn't want no surprises 'cause she doesn't like surprises.

T: She doesn't?

C: No. My baby doesn't like surprises. So she doesn't eat 'em up 'cause she doesn't like 'em.

T: She doesn't care about surprises anyway.

C: No. But she—. Yes, you do like surprises!

T: She really does, hm?

C: But she doesn't want no surprises. (*Continues to walk around room.*)

T: She's through with all those.

C: What a naughty baby!

T: Is she a naughty baby?

C: Yes, she's just a naughty baby.

T: I see.

C: And she's gonna get no surprise. And close her eyes, and close her eyes.

T: Shut her eyes, and no surprise.

C: Yes. (*Tugs at vise and pushes it back and forth.*) What a silly dumbbell I am.

T: Are you a silly dumbbell?

C: Yeah, I'm so silly. (*Pours some sand from dish into small bathtub. Then spills sand on rug.*) There! Spill that all on the rug.

T: Just spill it all over. That's the way you feel, hm?

C: (*Tosses tub aside. Picks up pieces of doll furniture and tosses them aside.*) I'll squeeze that out, and squeeze that out. And squeeze that out and squeeze that out.

T: Squeeze them all out.

C: And turn the squeezes out. And squeeze that out.

T: You want everything to be squeezed out.

C: (*Picks up part of the toy record player.*) This is a victrola. Squeeze that out. Squeeze that out. (*Continues to toss furniture to one side.*) I wanta go now.

T: Are you all finished, Kathy? You still have a few more mintues.

You can stay if you like. If you want to go, it's up to you.

C: I wanta stay.

T: You want to stay for a few more minutes?

C: Uh-huh.

T: All right. There're just about three more minutes.

C: (*Scrapes sand from table onto floor with paddle.*) I'm gonna spill this all on the floor.

T: You just want to spill it all on the floor, hm?

C: (*Stamps on the sand.*) Stamp! Stamp! (*Drops paddle on floor and runs across room.*) The wolf's here. I'm gonna run to my mommy.

T: Are you afraid the wolf is chasing you?

C: And he's not gonna get me. (*Picks up doll from mother's lap and kisses it. Holds it up in the air. Holds doll's legs around her neck.*) Upsy-daisy. Upsy-daisy.

T: You want to hold her real tight, hm?

C: No. Just take her upsy-daisy.

T: Oh.

C: Upsy-daisy. Upsy-daisy. Upsy-daisy. Upsy-daisy. She likes to go up.

T: Well, Kathy, our time is just about up for today.

C: O.K. (*Throws doll on the floor.*) Let's go, Mom. Good-by.

T: Good-by, Kathy.

C: Good-by.

Discussion: December 20 Play Session

Again Kathy expresses her fears directly, running to her mother and claiming "the wolf" is chasing her. She shows anger toward her father, retaliating in kind to his methods: "He'll have to go to bed with no surprises . . . 'cause he wasn't good . . . so to bed with him without anything." She refuses to give her daddy a glass of water or a good-night kiss in the play sequences. She decides to give her mother the surprises and "all the presents." She rationalizes her own position with, "I don't want any surprises," and resists the pressures, refusing to eat dinner, surprises or no surprises. This scene is played out repeatedly.

In a new role Kathy's hostility mounts. She spills water on the rug without concern. She attempts to crush various pieces of toy furniture, throws sand on the floor, and stamps her feet on the floor. These expressions of generalized anger are followed by fear. She runs to her mother and says "the wolf" is chasing her. In a final gesture she throws the baby doll on the floor and leaves.

Kathy's primary use of the play therapy experience seems to be an ever-further expression and exploration of her attitudes of fear and anger.

December 22. Telephone Conversation with Father

F: Oh, brother! What a mess! I think I had better see you and tell you a few things. I don't know what to do or say. Have you got any ideas? She'll get up at eight in the morning. She's so tired. We put her to bed, and she will not sleep. She calls her mother. She cries something fierce. Last night she wasn't getting on my nerves like she used to, even though she was interrupting our sleep.

A couple of nights ago she was still talking. I said, "Kathy, get out of bed if you don't sleep." She refuses to sleep. She wakes up at twelve-thirty or one, and when she wakes up, she's fully awake. Maybe I am seeing more than is really there. When she yawns, it isn't a full yawn. It's a forced one, and it's a fight against sleep. Like last night she didn't sleep well. She won't sleep through the night. Sometimes I feel like saying, "Kathy, you go to sleep."

It makes me feel very, very bad to see her like that. I realize that it was bad to try to make her perfect. Well, I'll come in and see you next week.

December 27. Interview with Father

F: The day I called you, my inside was in a turmoil, and I guess it's because Kathy was worse that day and the day before. When she starts to relax, then it shows more, and I feel better.

T: When she gets worse, then it makes you feel worse, is that it?

F: I know it is wrong to think that way. She gets better and then she gets worse and then gets better again and worse again. But each time the better is stronger and the worse is weaker. I think at that moment things will start slacking.

T: It's a kind of unsteady process, then.

F: Sometimes I think it will fade, and sometimes I don't. The little son of a gun—she's so hard to figure out. It's going away, and I know it will. I think at that moment it's going to get better, and then it gets worse. Then when it seems hopeless, it gets better again.

T: It's really a puzzling matter then, isn't it?

F: I'll tell you a couple more incidents. (*Pause.*) This morning Kathy woke up early, as she often does, and she got into bed with Dee. It so happens our bedroom faces a road, and as the cars go by, they throw a passing shadow, and that's her bugaboo—any kind of shadow. She put her head on the pillow and didn't want to see the shadow. I said, "Come downstairs, Kathy, and talk to me. I have to go to work." She looked on the front window at the door. She glanced at it several times. I said, "Honey, do you know what a shadow is?" There were some shadows on the front room floor, so I took my hand and made shadows and said, "See, honey, the shadow is my hand," and I said, "Now you put your hand like that." A little later she yelled, "Ma," and told her what she saw. When I left for work I sensed it made no difference with her. She was still afraid of the shadows.

Last night after supper she started going down the basement, and halfway down she came back and said, "The train was chasing me." Dee said, "What would happen if the train caught you?" and she said, "It would make me dead," and I said, "Not while we're here." These things are funny with her. Her fears of the shadows—she laughs while talking about it, but I notice that she's dead serious.

Now I'm getting a little nervous. Maybe it's talking about all this that makes me that way. Another thing, let me tell you. I stay with her now. She feels more secure with me in the room on the daybed. Instead of trying to make her stay by herself, I stay with her. Last night I told her two stories.

You remember the first time I came to see you, I was in one mess. I didn't know what to do. It seems as if she's gotten a lot better. At least she talks about it and tells you what she's afraid of. Dee asked her, "What would happen if the train did catch you?" and now she answers, but before she wouldn't. I would say she has improved. I have a right to feel I can't help myself in the way I think or act.

T: You do things because you have to do them.

F: I know where I failed. I failed to realize that I always thought Kathy to be abnormal, for instance. She eternally wanted to sit on my lap and do what I do. I see other kids are the same way. I realize that it is normal for a child to show so much affection.

T: For a while you were afraid she showed too much love, but now you accept it as normal.

F: I felt she was just sitting on my lap too much, and now I'm beginning to realize that it is her search for security. I'd like to ask you a question between you and me. Did you not say that she has to learn to accept some things? I feel that it is a lot of security to her. I think it is excellent, whether she shows fears or not. I was in a mess that day, but since then I calmed down. After Kathy was in bed, we sort of joked about it. Eventually she'll be the same.

Do you feel, now you know us, do you think that it's both of us? Or do you think that it's just me? That's what's bothering us. We don't know what's behind the fears. We don't know who it is.

I'll tell you what transpired. I was very decisive with her. I just did things. Whether it was right or wrong, I went ahead and told her. I thought she didn't make up her own mind. I felt she's getting away from it to a great degree. She's not a dumb kid. She can use us like mad. Another thing, too. I have told you before when we put the supper on the table she would say, "I don't want it. I don't like it." We say to her, "You sit there until you're ready." She sits for a minute, but then she usually eats it. I think there's a definite improvement. Several things point to it. One thing, she talks about it. She's not indecisive. She doesn't switch. I wish we had ten more like her.

T: You really love her, don't you?

F: Oh, she's a wonderful kid. Basically, she's such a good girl.

Dee drags her everywhere, and not a peep out of her. We feel we've got one in a million.

T: You think the world of her.

F: I've gotten away—my sister has told me I am a perfectionist. I don't know whether that started the fears, but I don't want her perfect. I don't expect her to be perfect. A child can't be perfect. It is very far from perfect. Those things I never realized before. I have never had a child before. Now I know. In other words, whatever the child does, let the child do. I don't give a damn if she walks up and down the stairs with something in her arms, but after she goes to the toilet and comes out with her pants down, I do expect her to pull them up.

T: That's pretty upsetting, isn't it?

F: I noticed something else I meant to tell you. Sometimes I'm upstairs, and she'll want to come downstairs, and she'll say, "Mommy, I want to take your hand to come downstairs." She'll start to act like she's getting fears. She'll insist in a crying way that it would be her life.

  She started crying once, and I blew up and slapped her on the rear, and then she went downstairs by herself. If I am going down when she is, then I'll take her, but otherwise she'll have to go down herself. She might have been upstairs for a reason, and she'll want Dee to take her hand, or she'll finally reach a compromise. Dee will say, "Come to the bottom and I'll catch you toward the bottom." I love her. I just love the hell out of her.

T: Your feelings for her are very strong.

F: They couldn't be any stronger. It stems from the fact that I would have such a gorgeous child, such a beautiful kid. To us, she's beautiful. I never thought I would have anything so wonderful. Dee loves her just as much as I do.

T: You both love her very much.

F: I couldn't find any more happiness with anyone else on this earth. Dee's love gives me the security I need. It is her undivided, unrestrained relationship with me. She overlooks so many things in me.

T: You really appreciate the way she overlooks your faults.

F: Absolutely. We don't show too much affection in front of Kathy. As a matter of fact, Dee bawls me out because I have been kissing Kathy a lot and not her.

T: Perhaps you feel you love Kathy too much.

F: No, I don't. I show Kathy all the affection in the world. I pick her up a thousand times, and I play with her. Dee shows her all the affection in the world, too. Since the fears, I feel that I have to show Kathy more affection. I've grown into the idea that if I try to show her more love, it will help Kathy do away with her fears. I could never show her too much affection. Of course, there is a point, if she hangs on to you night and day when she could be doing other things. Then I insist that she do them. I don't think it would be possible to have too much love. I lacked it myself, the affection part. There couldn't be anything there—not too much of that for a child. I never knew that children could have fears as they do. I'm getting less and less worried about it, and maybe that's helping, too.

January 3. Play Session with Kathy

C: I can run real, real, real fast.

T: You're a fast runner, hm?

C: See? (*Runs out into hall and then runs back into room.*)

T: Yes.

C: (*Runs in and out of hall again.*)

T: You really like to run then, don't you?

C: Yes. (*Continues to run back and forth.*) I like to run better than walk. I like to run better.

T: Than walking?

C: Yes. (*Stares at hall.*) A big wolf.

T: Is there a big wolf out there?

C: (*Hands T two puppets.*) You're gonna get these puppets. And Mommy's gonna have these. They aren't the same color. (*Hands two puppets to mother.*) These are so furry. (*Kneels by sandbox. Fills bowl with sand and chops it with a spoon.*) Mommy has a chopping bowl. She uses a big bowl. (*Handles sand.*) You know, when I get undressed for bed, Daddy always brings me surprises.

T: Daddy always brings you surprises when you get undressed for bed?

C: No. He doesn't bring me surprises when I go to sleep at night. He always gives me surprises at dinner. (*Stands up and hands mother a balloon.*) Mommy's gonna get this balloon 'cause she was a good girl, and you're not.

T: I'm bad, hm?

C: Because you were cranky all day.

T: Cranky all day long.

C: (*Spills sand on the floor.*)

T: It really spilled all over.

C: I gotta find my chopping bowl.

T: Where did the chopping bowl go?

C: All the time I say pooh. Pooh, pooh, pooh.

T: That's just what you feel like saying: pooh.

C: When Donna used to hit me, I used to hit her back real hard. When she hits me I'll hit her real, real hard. I'll pour a drink of water down her throat.

T: That's what you'll do, so she better watch out.

C: Yeah. (*Runs around the room. Picks up large father doll, then drops it on the floor.*) Throw the little squeaky away.

T: You're throwing it away. You don't care about that.

C: Throwing everything away.

T: You don't like any of them.

C: No. I don't like any of them. (*Tosses a few more toys aside. Picks up shovel and bowl from floor and moves to sandbox. Handles sand.*) Mr. C, you remember I told you when Donna used to throw sand in my eyes?

T: Mm-hm.

C: That made me unhappy. Mommy had to put water in my eyes.

T: That really made you unhappy.

C: Yes. I was unhappy. (*Moves away from sandbox and kicks ball around the room. Pushes comeback. Picks up doll and feeds it with small bottle.*) This has water in it. Drink it. She likes water. She wants it out of the big bottle. (*Picks up large bottle and hands it to T.*) Take the top off. How do you turn it?

T: See?

C: Let me try.

T: It came right off, didn't it?

C: (*Empties small bottle of water into large bottle. Handles the doll.*) It's time for the baby to take her bath. She doesn't like to take her bath.

T: She doesn't like that, does she?

C: No. But she's gonna take one. She doesn't like to stay up by herself. (*Stuffs doll's diaper into large bottle.*) Baby doesn't like to take her bath.

T: She has to do it anyway.

C: (*Washes the doll with wet diaper.*) I don't care when I take a bath. I like to take a bath.

T: It doesn't bother you at all.

C: No.

T: The baby just doesn't like it.

C: She just has to take a bath. She's been like that for three months.

T: Three months she's been like that, hm?

C: Yes. Make her very clean. She's very, very dirty. Her feet are very, very dirty. Wipe her tooshy off. (*Bottle of water overturns. Pours remaining water in bottle over doll.*) Now she had a good bath. Now she's going to bed. Get her slippers. Baby's going to bed. You're in your own bed. You have to close your eyes.

T: She has to close her eyes now.

C: I have a bigger bed than hers. It's nighttime. Go to sleep. (*Places doll on the bench, then lies down on bench.*) I have to sleep next to her.

T: Now you and the baby are going to sleep together.

C: Yes. (*Pulls another bench next to hers and places doll on that one.*) I've got a real, real big bed. The baby got a real, real little bed.

T: And you're both going to sleep.

C: Yes. I don't care if I stay in here all day.

T: You don't? Well, there is still fifteen minutes left.

C: I'll stay here another fifteen minutes.

T: O.K.

C: I'm a good actor. Aunty Emma's a bad actor. (*Stands up and fills bowl with sand. Chops sand with shovel.*) Mommy's a good actor, and Aunty Emma's a bad girl. She has a big house. Old houses make me sad.

T: Old houses make you sad?

C: Old houses certainly do make me sad.

T: Are you a sad girl?

C: Yes. Because I don't like sad houses. (*Pretends to feed doll some sand.*) Take this, baby. Take it. O.K., take it. See how you like it. Put it back in the bowl. Baby doesn't like chopped liver. I don't want to make no more chopped liver.

T: You don't want to make what baby doesn't eat.

C: Mommy doesn't make the same kind chopped liver. I like chopped liver. Mommy doesn't make this kind.

T: She makes the kind you like.

C: This kind is pooey. Chopped liver is all ready. Put this on the table. (*Empties some water into bowl of sand and rubs sand all over doll's body.*) I never want to play with this again, Mommy.

M: Why not?

C: Because I get myself all dirty. Now baby has to eat. Have to get a towel now. (*Runs to doorway and looks at mother.*) You come with me. (*Mother and C walk out to bathroom.*)

Discussion: January 3 Play Session

Kathy's positive feelings toward her father return. She says, "You know, when I get undressed for bed, Daddy always brings me surprises." There is also some ambivalence. Kathy picks up the father-doll figure and throws it hard on the floor.

Kathy reenacts the feeding situation, emphasizing that when she does not want to eat something, she will refuse.

JANUARY 10. PLAY SESSION WITH KATHY

C: (*Comes into room and pulls chair from around side of workbench. Sits down and pats at clay with stick.*) Get me some water, Mom.

T: You want Mommy to do it for you.

C: Yes. I'll get the other water then. (*Carries clay to pail of water and wets it.*) There.

T: Mm-hm.

C: Mommy, get me some water.

T: You want more water.

C: Mommy, I want some water.

M: You can get some water yourself, honey.

C: No, I can't!

M: You try.

C: No, you give me some. (*Hands mother the bowl.*)

T: You just want to tell Mommy what to do, hm?

M: Look, I'll show you. (*Mother fills bowl with water from pail. Hands bowl to C, who spills water out of it.*)

C: I want it full. That's not full.

M: You want more water in there? All right. Now you can do it yourself. Here.

C: I want some more.

M: There's this one way you can take it.

C: I want you to get some more out of the sink.

M: No, you get it from here, honey.

C: But there's not enough water. I need some water out of the sink. 'Cause that's not enough!

T: You're pretty mad about it, hm?

C: 'Cause I don't like that kind.

T: You don't like it out of the pail.

C: No, I don't. 1 just like it from the sink.

T: Mm-hm.

C: (*Fills bowl and slowly carries it to workbench. Sits in chair and pats clay with stick.*) I'm gonna mash it. You just watch what I'm gonna do.

T: O.K.

C: I'm cooking dinner. (*Picks up spoon and jabs at clay with it.*) By the time I get home, my hands will be all dirty. You know, Mr. C?

T: Mm-hm. That's what you're going to do, hm? Get them all dirty.

C: But I won't like that.

T: Don't you like to have your hands dirty?

C: No! It makes me unhappy when I have my hands all dirty. But it doesn't. It doesn't make me unhappy when I get my hands all dirty. I'm gonna make my dolly clean. Where's my cute little dolly? The one with the diaper.

T: Where is she?

C: Here she is! She wants to take a bath. (*Takes off diaper and lets doll fall on the floor.*) Now the diaper has to get washed. (*Dips diaper into bowl of water and rubs it slowly over the clay.*) I just came here. I don't wanta go home now, 'cause I just came here.

T: You have a lot of things you want to do.

C: (*Picks up doll and handles it with clay-covered hands.*) She has to get real clean, 'cause I told her to. She wants to get clean. I'm gonna wash her. (*Rubs hands with clay and "washes" doll with paper towel.*) I'll get you all cleaned up. All cleaned up. My hands are all full of that stuff. She's gonna get all cleaned for a birthday party. She's going to a birthday party today. You know? You know, Mommy? My baby's going to a birthday party today.

M: Mm-hm.

C: (*Rubs paper towel over clay and wipes it on doll.*) Her hair is dirty. Her eyes are dirty. And I'm gonna wash her eyes too. You know where Daddy works? Daddy works at ———— Company. (*Pause.*) My baby doesn't know how to clean herself. All the time she makes me wash her. She likes me to wash her, 'cause she doesn't know how. All the time she has dirty feet and dirty hands. Now, baby, I'm gonna put you in clean water. In dry water. (*Puts doll into pail of water. Pushes it back and forth in pail.*) Washy-washy, swimmy-swimmy. Swimmy-swimmy, swimmy-swimmy. Get a wash cloth. Clean her off. (*Brings paper towel from workbench and rubs doll vigorously with towel.*) I'll clean her off. Now she's all through taking a bath. I'm gonna dry her. She's soaking wet. (*Marches around the room holding doll. Places doll in sandbox. Steps into box and crouches in sand.*) She wants to lay in the sand so she can play.

T: Mm-hm.

C: I'm gonna stand in the sand.

T: Mm-hm.

C: With my good shoes on. These are my good shoes. (*Walks around in sandbox.*)

T: And you're standing in the sand with them, hm?

C: I'll keep 'em on. I hope I don't get sand in 'em 'cause they're my good shoes.

T: Mm-hm.

C: (*Steps out of the sandbox and picks up a hand puppet.*) This bad guy can eat my mommy up.

T: Oh.

C: I don't like that.

T: Don't you like your mommy to be eaten up?

C: No. 'Cause who will take care of him when he goes to work —my daddy?

T: Who would take care of your daddy then, hm?

C: Daddy isn't the girlie. Throw the bad guy away. I'll throw him in the dirt of water. Yeah, I'll throw him in the water. (*Tosses puppet into pail of water.*)

T: That's for the bad guy. Into the water.

C: Yes. Into the water. I don't care if he gets wet. And I'll paintbrush with this. (*Pushes puppet around in pail with a paintbrush.*)

T: That'll take care of him.

C: Yes. (*Continues to push puppet with paintbrush. Picks up another brush and jabs at puppet.*) First this stick, then the other stick.

T: You'll use two for him.

C: He's eating up by a bad guy. He's gonna be eaten up. I'll show him. And it's off to bed he goes. And I'm not gonna bring home no surprise for this bad guy. No surprise. Into the water with this bad guy.

T: Nothing for him, hm?

C: Nothing. No supper for him. Into the water with him. (*Lifts puppet out of pail with brush and then lets it drop back into pail. Stirs puppet in the water.*)

T: You're really giving him some pretty bad treatment.

C: Yeah. I wanta get all his clothes all wet.

T: Mm-hm.

C: Now he's going down the drain and down the drain. You'll see him down the drain. 'Cause he's gonna eat me up.

T: He's getting everything he deserves, hm?

C: Yes. He even puts me in the water and bangs me down the drain.

T: Is that what he does to you?

C: Yes. But I'm gonna do it to him. I'm gonna drain him down the drain.

T: He'll get just what he gives you, hm?

C: Yes. He's going down and down the drain. (*Throws another puppet into the pail.*) This guy is bad, so I have to drain him down the drain. Most of the guys are mean to me. This guy is mean to me. (*Throws doll from sandbox into pail.*) Every guy is mean to me. Every guy I have to drain down the drain. Every guy is mean to me.

T: Every guy is mean to you.

C: Yes, everyone. Everyone is going down the drain. (*Stirs figures in pail with brush.*)

T: So you're going to be mean to them.

C: Yes. Everybody drains down the drain. 'Cause everybody drains me down the drain. Everybody doesn't like me.

T: Nobody likes you, hm?

C: All the time my hair gets dirty. I don't like that. Shame on them. They're gonna go to breakfast, but nothing for supper. No, I won't give them anything.

T: You won't give them a single thing, hm?

C: Yes. Now look here. This is the only thing they're gonna get. See? This is the only thing. (*Drops clay into pail of water.*) They're going down the drain.

T: You'll give them plenty of that, won't you?

C: (*Pokes at figures in pail with brush.*) Now how do you like that? Isn't that nice? They're going down the drain, down the drain, and down the drain. How do you like that guy? You have to go down the drain, 'cause I want you to.

T: You want him to go down the drain.

C: All of them are going down the drain. Going down the drain and down the drain. Stick them back down in the water. I'll cut 'em with a knife. With a knife. (*Throws a rubber knife into the pail.*) Stick a knife in the water. That's gonna be very sharp.

T: They're liable to get cut up with that, hm?

C: Here's a gun. This is a ladder. Here's a hammer. And here's a gun! (*Tosses more items into pail. Starts to throw tractor in also but replaces it on table. Stirs items in pail with brush.*) Everybody is mean to me. They don't like me. Everybody don't like me. They're all mean to me.

T: Everyone is so mean to you.

C: Yes. The truck is mean to me. Everyone is mean to me. The car is mean to me. Everybody'll drown down the drain.

T: When they're mean to you, that's what you'll do to them.

C: Everybody is so mean to me.

T: Nobody likes you, hm?

C: No! So I'm gonna drain 'em down the drain and drain 'em down the drain. I'll get more water and spill 'em down the drain. (*Empties bowl of water into pail.*) There. Now you're gonna get real sad, and I'll like that.

T: Will you be glad when they're real sad and unhappy?

C: Yes! 'Cause I like 'em to.

T: Mm-hm.

C: Get everything off. This old truck. This gun. (*Throws toys from table on the floor.*)

T: Everything goes, hm?

C: Everything. Everyone is mean to me today. The telephone's ringing. The telephone is dirty. Up and down the numbers. I'm making the numbers wet. (*Dips brush into bottle of water and rubs it over telephone dial.*)

T: Are the numbers naughty, too?

C: They're naughty. The numbers are naughty to me, too. They're naughty to me. That's why I have to make 'em up and down. (*Dips brush into bottle and continues to wet telephone dial.*)

T: This is one time you're going to teach them a lesson.

C: One time I'm gonna teach 'em a lesson. When they get nicer to me, then I'm gonna teach 'em a good lesson. Now how you like that? Now I'm gonna see if I can talk. (*Carries telephone to mother's lap. Holds receiver to ear.*) Hello,

Aunty Joan. Hello. Hello. It's my puppet. My dear puppet. It's my dear puppet.

M: Hello, dear puppet.

C: Talk.

M: Oh, I don't know what to say to your puppet. You talk to him.

C: No! I'm not gonna do anything for him. (*Takes telephone from mother and continues to brush it.*) You know what he loves? You know what he told me? He loves me. He loves me. With kisses.

T: Is that what he does? He gives you so many kisses because he loves you?

C: Mm-hm. But Aunty Emma is a bad girl.

T: She is?

C: Yes.

T: You don't like her, hm?

C: I'm gonna kick her. And this time I'm gonna kick her.

T: That's what you feel like doing to her, hm?

C: Yes. 'Cause she's a bad girl. I'm gonna hit her over the head.

T: Wow! You're really going to give it to her, aren't you?

C: Yes. 'Cause she's a bad girl, and I don't like her. I don't want to see her any more.

T: You don't?

C: No. (*Handles telephone and paintbrush.*) I'll just have to get a telephone and kick her.

T: You must feel pretty mad at her.

C: 'Cause I don't like her. Mommy doesn't feel mad at Aunty Emma.

T: She doesn't, but you do.

C: Yes. (*Picks up sieve and paints it with water.*) I'm just gonna paint you something. Watch what I'm gonna paint. I'm gonna paint all these toys a different color.

T: You want to change everything around today, don't you?

C: Yes. There's gonna be a birthday party today. It's dolly's birthday party today. Baby always cries when she doesn't have a birthday party. Baby doesn't have a friend when she doesn't have a birthday party.

T: She must be very sad, then.

C: Yes. She's gonna get a birthday party and cookies and nothing

else. 'Cause she's a bad girl. She didn't listen to what I say.
(*Takes doll out of pail and holds it.*)

T: You mean when she doesn't listen to what you tell her, then
she doesn't get things, hm?

C: No coffee and no tea and no nothing. She's going to bed with
nothing. I'm gonna throw all of them in the fire. The fire's
right out over here. (*Walks to door and throws doll into
outer hall.*) There, baby. Now the other kids. (*Throws two
puppets into hall.*)

T: You'll throw them all in the fire. Let them burn.

C: This one goes in the fire. The fireman's gonna come and take
them away. And throw them away in a fire.

T: They'll be all finished up, won't they?

C: I don't like that. I don't like the way they did that. They're
gonna get a birthday party. And I said I'm not gonna eat
my lunch. (*Walks to vise and turns handle.*) Babies don't
like to be burned in the fire.

T: They don't like to be burned, but they are.

C: Yes, but they're burned. I throw mine in the fire. The garbage
man's gonna come and put 'em away in a truck. I'm gonna
put cuckoo—. I'm gonna make pissy on him. Come on,
cuckoo. I'm gonna make pissy on you. (*Goes to doorway
and pulls down her pants. Pulls them up again and walks
back into room.*) I made pissy on him.

T: You made pissy on him, hm?

C: Yes.

T: That's what you did. You felt like doing it, so you did.

C: Here's another wolf. (*Goes to doorway again and pulls down
pants, then pulls them up.*) There.

T: You really are taking care of the wolves today. You pissied
right on them.

C: Yes. (*Touches puppets on mother's lap.*) I love these with fur.
These are good. They listen to what I say. (*Takes puppets
and places them on bench. Lies down on bench, holding
puppets.*) They really want to sleep in my bed. They really
want to sleep in my bed tonight.

T: They really want to sleep with you.

C: Here comes the flutter. (*Gets up and runs to mother and leans against her. Looks at T.*) Out came the flutter looking for me. My mommy. Then the flutter comes to hit me.

T: Are you afraid of the flutter?

C: Yes.

T: So you run to your mother.

C: Yes. I'm gonna go get my bench. (*Walks to bench and looks at it. Then runs back to mother.*) There's no more flutter-bies.

T: No more flutterbies. They're all gone.

C: There's no more. (*Walks to middle of room, then back to mother.*) They weren't all gone.

T: They weren't? There are some there that still bother you, aren't there?

C: There are some nice ones who take care of the bad flutterbies. There's some good flutterbies.

T: There are good flutterbies and bad flutterbies.

C: And the good are—. The king don't like me.

T: Doesn't the king like you?

C: But he always trusts me. I could stay up all night.

T: Is that why you stay up all night?

C: Yes. Oh, splash. (*Throws bottle on the floor and it breaks. Looks startled.*)

T: Well, we'll have to sweep it away so you won't cut yourself, Kathy. I'll just put it out of the way like this now.

C: Now I wanta lay down. (*Stretches out on table, lying on her stomach.*)

T: Now you're really going to lay down, hm?

C: I really have to lay down. This is my good dress.

T: Mm-hm. Is that the way you like to sleep?

C: Yes. (*Lies on table quietly.*)

T: That's about all the time we have left today, Kathy.

C: I'll be back. Don't forget your coat, Mommy. Good-by.

T: Good-by, Kathy.

Discussion: January 10 Play Session

Kathy attempts to get her mother to do things for her, but her mother, unlike previous times, makes Kathy's responsibilities clear. Her ambivalence about cleanliness is shown in her statement, "It makes me unhappy when I have my hands all dirty. But it doesn't make me unhappy when I get my hands all dirty." She still scrubs the baby doll thoroughly.

Kathy throws the "bad guy" into the pail of water and says, "He's gonna be eaten up." She attempts to push the "bad guy" down the drain. The negative feelings are expanded as she expresses a wish to throw all the human figures down the drain. She exclaims that people are mean to her so she is forced to retaliate. Her feelings increase in intensity as she says, "I'll cut 'em all with a knife. With a knife." She shouts, "Everybody is mean to me. They don't like me. Everybody don't like me. They're all mean to me." This is repeated again and again.

Positive perceptions of her father are perhaps indicated in her comments on the male puppet, "He loves me. He loves me. With kisses." Kathy expresses feelings of resentment toward an aunt, saying, "Aunty Emmy is a bad girl . . . I'm gonna kick her . . . I'm gonna hit her over the head."

At the end of the session Kathy shows strength against two of her fears, "the cuckoo" and "the wolf." She pulls down her pants and says, "There. I made pissy on them."

JANUARY 11. TELEPHONE CONVERSATION WITH FATHER

F: Dee wanted me to call you and tell you of an incident that happened in class—the part where she chased a wolf and lowered her pants nicely and sissied on it. She got that from a girl friend. I thought you might want to know that.

She is going to bed nicely lately. She always wants me to tell her the story of Little Red Riding Hood. She always wants to hear about the wolf chasing Red Riding Hood and the part where the father kills the wolf with an ax.

She has no fears about the signs any more. I think she's made terrific progress. It makes it much better in our household. She's a cutie. She's got a whole bunch of personality, and she's got brains in her head. We love her so much, and we laugh our heads off with her. In other words, things are going back to a normal shape. Before, we used to be frightened when she talked kind of silly, but now we just laugh with her, and we all have a good time about it. Do you see any point in her continuing to come?

T: Well, I think we should let her make that decision.

F: O.K., then. Whenever she decides that she's had enough, then we'll stop.

JANUARY 17. PLAY SESSION WITH KATHY

C: (*Runs into the room and picks up a balloon.*) You're gonna get the biggest balloon, Mr. C.

T: I'm going to get the biggest one?

C: This is the biggest.

T: O.K.

C: (*Picks up small gun.*) Mommy. (*Walks around the room.*) That bad guy is gonna shoot me. (*Picks up a puppet.*)

T: He is?

C: So you know that's to bed with him. (*Tosses puppet into pail of water.*)

T: Oh, he's going right down into bed.

C: Yes. 'Cause he's so stupid. And so naughty.

T: He's naughty and stupid, hm?

C: And this one is a naughty one. (*Throws another puppet into pail.*) And everyone.

T: Everybody's naughty today, hm?

C: This one, and the horsie is naughty. (*Throws small doll and horse figure into pail.*) Everybody is naughty today.

T: Just a lot of naughty people.

C: Yes. (*Tosses flat figure balloon into pail.*) That stupid old guy! Every time I see him. He's so stupid.

T: He's stupid all the time.

C: Everybody's mean to me. I'm gonna step on him and be an ogre. (*Turns head of Mickey Mouse tractor, then tosses it into pail.*) Put some stuff in his eyes. He was driving.

T: So he's naughty, too.

C: Everybody! (*Picks up animal puppets and hugs them.*) These are the good ones.

T: Mm-hm. Those are the nice ones.

C: Yes. You hold them, Mommy. (*Picks up a balloon and jumps up and down.*) Jing. I'm gonna sing you a song. First I have to sit down like the girl who is teaching the song. (*Sits down in chair.*)

T: Mm-hm.

C: (*Jumps up from chair and stands near mother.*) You know something? This is gonna be "Jingle Bells."

T: You like that song.

C: Yes. (*Sings "Jingle Bells."*) Always like to dance. (*Sits on chair next to workbench. Dips paintbrush into bottle of water, then smears it on paper.*) I'm pretending I'm painting a house.

T: O.K.

C: You know what house I'm gonna paint? This is gonna be a pink one. It will be a different one.

T: It will be different from any other house, hm?

C: Yes. (*Hums. Rubs brush on clay, then dabs it on paper.*) See what house this is gonna be? See?

T: Mm-hm.

C: (*Hums. Pokes brush into piece of clay.*) I'm pretending that I'm mashing some potatoes.

T: Mm-hm.

C: You remember Daddy?

T: Mm-hm.

C: Larry!

T: I remember him.

C: (*Kneels on chair and looks at T.*) You don't know his last name. His last name is B!

T: Mm-hm.

C: And Mommy's last name is Mrs. B! You know?

T: They both have the same last name, hm?

C: No!

T: They don't?

C: Daddy's last name is B.

T: Oh.

C: Do you have the record of "Get Out of Here"?

T: No.

C: I do. My daddy just bought it on Saturday. Do you know that? 'Cause I really like that song.

T: And were you happy about that?

C: Yes, I was so happy to hear it. And I danced and I danced and I danced till the song was over. Then I played it again.

T: It really made you feel good, didn't it?

C: Yes. (*Sits in chair again. Dips brush in bottle, then on clay. Brushes some clay on paper.*) I'm making a picture for you. A pretty one. I'm painting a picture for you.

T: Mm-hm.

C: I like you! That's why I'm painting you a picture.

T: Oh, I see.

C: If you were an aunt, then I wouldn't like you. If you were an aunt.

T: You wouldn't like me if I were an aunt?

C: No. (*Handles paper and clay.*) You know what I'm making? A house!

T: You're making a house, hm? Just what you want to do.

C: Yes. (*Pause.*) That's what I'm making.

T: You seem to like to make houses.

C: I really like to make houses. I feel like it.

T: You feel like making houses?

C: Yes. (*Continues to handle brush and clay. Pokes holes into clay with brush.*) I have to be real quiet, 'cause the cuckoo strikes midnight. Dong! Every time I play with Marcia the cuckoo strikes midnight. Every time I play with Marcia I go to sleep when it's midnight. You know that, Mr. C? And every time the cuckoo strikes midnight when it's morningtime. She's only pretending.

T: Oh, I see. But you go to sleep when she pretends.

C: Yes, when the cuckoo strikes midnight. All the time she says it's morningtime.

T: Mm-hm. She does some pretty funny things, doesn't she?

C: Yes. Every time Marcia says the cuckoo strikes midnight, she says, "Go to sleep." 'Cause the cuckoo strikes midnight, and I say "No." And she says, "Do you wanta get hurt?" No.

T: She told you you'd get hurt if you didn't, hm?

C: (*Pauses. Hums.*) Oh, the cuckoo strikes midnight! (*Runs to mother and hugs her.*)

T: The cuckoo really struck midnight, hm?

C: Yes, the cuckoo struck. I wanta sit on your lap. (*Sits on mother's lap.*) Oh, lookit my hands.

M: Oh, my goodness.

C: (*Looks at T.*) You know what, Daddy? You know what? Oh! I forgot the wrong name! (*Laughs.*)

T: Mm-hm. You really forgot that time, didn't you?

C: I forgot and said "Daddy." I forgot and said the wrong name.

T: Mm-hm.

C: (*Moves away from mother and picks up jump rope. Twirls it.*) Oh! The cuckoo strikes midnight! (*Runs to mother.*)

T: When the cuckoo strikes midnight, then you run, hm?

C: Yes. (*Sits on mother's lap.*) I don't want Mommy to breathe.

T: Oh, you just want Mommy to stop breathing altogether.

C: Mm-hm. If she doesn't stop, I'll dump her in there in the water and make her sweater get all wet.

T: Is that what you'd like to do?

C: Yes.

T: Dump her right down and get her all wet.

C: (*Picks up jump rope.*) Now, now, I'll just swing it around.

T: You make it go round and round.

C: You know, I won't stop swinging this, 'cause the people go round and round in circles jumping rope.

T: People do funny things sometimes, don't they?

C: Yes. Swingy, swingy. (*Continues to twirl rope while sitting on mother's lap.*) I just love that song. "All I Want for Christmas is My Two Front Teeth"—I like that song.

T: Mm-hm.

C: I'm swinging the rope around. I wanta swing it over my leg. (*Drops rope and stands up to get it. Wants to sit on mother's lap again.*) Up again. I want to get up again.

M: Oh, honey, you're getting heavy.

T: You want to sit right on Mommy's lap.

C: Don't want to move for three weeks.

T: You're not going to move for three weeks, hm?

C: I'm not gonna talk about it.

T: O.K.

C: (*Handles jump rope.*) Oh, the cuckoo strikes midnight! Don't want the cuckoo to strike midnight.

T: Are you afraid of the cuckoo striking midnight?

C: Yes. (*Hands jump rope to mother.*) Hold it like this. Like this, Mommy, so the cuckoo won't strike. The cuckoo is falling. (*Takes rope from mother.*) When he hears the cuckoo strike midnight, he runs out of this room.

T: He's afraid of the cuckoo.

C: Yes, he is. I'm stopping the cuckoo. (*Continues to twirl the rope.*)

T: As long as you do that, then the cuckoo stops, hm?

C: Yes. I hear the cuckoo knocking on the window. Knock, knock. I see an ogre gonna eat me up. I'm gonna keep striking this, and the clock is gonna stop. And there's a hoke coming to catch the cuckoo, and he's gonna kill the cuckoo with a stick.

T: And there'll be no more cuckoo, then.

C: (*Drops rope and picks it up. Sits on mother's lap again.*)

T: Mommy's having quite a struggle keeping you on her lap.

C: Yes. (*Swings jump rope vigorously.*) Cuckoo! Cuckoo, get out of here! I'll make the clock strike, and the cuckoo's gonna eat the ogre up. Dum-dum-dum. Da-da-da-da-da-da. The cuckoo strikes midnight.

T: Mm-hm. You don't like the cuckoo.

C: No. I don't like the ogre, either. I'm gonna get rid of them. (*Swings rope.*) I got rid of the cuckoo and the ogre.

T: You got rid of them both.

C: Let's pretend you're Mom, and you're Daddy, and my other daddy—. I'm gonna pretend I'm Mommy, and you're Daddy, and Daddy's Donna C. (*Looks at T.*)

T: Daddy's Donna C.

C: And do you know Donna C?

T: I only know what you've talked about.

C: Well, I won't talk about her. I'm crumpling the rope up. (*Pulls mother's arm closer around her.*) Do I got a couple more minutes?

T: Oh yes, you still have a few more minutes.

C: But I don't want to stay here.

T: You don't want to stay?

C: No. I want to go home, then.

T: You can go home when you want to.

C: I'll stay a few more minutes. (*Pause.*) You know what? Mommy doesn't drive very good.

T: She doesn't?

C: Remember when she smashed the headlights? That's why I have to sit in the back.

T: Mm-hm.

C: (*Hums and handles jump rope.*) I'm gonna show you I can throw you a kiss.

T: Oh, I see.

C: (*Drops jump rope and picks it up.*) All the time the cuckoo strikes midnight. (*Wants to sit on mother's lap again.*)

M: Now you stand here, Kathy.

C: No, no!

M: You want to sit on my lap?

C: Yes.

M: Oh, Kathy. You're getting heavy, honey.

C: (*Sits on mother's lap.*) O.K. (*Points to ball on floor.*) Is this your ball?

T: It belongs in the playroom.

C: I want to take a balloon. Can I take a balloon home?

T: You really want to take one home, Kathy, but all the things have to stay in the room.

C: Why? Why?

T: You wonder why that's necessary.

C: Why, Mr. C?

T: Well, so the other children can play with them. And you can have them to play with next time you come.

C: Next time it'll be here when I come?

T: Mm-hm.

C: When can I go home?

T: You can go home whenever you want to, Kathy. You decide that.

C: Hold me real close.

T: Kathy just wants to be held by Mommy real, real close. Is that it, Kathy?

C: Mm-hm. (*Gets off mother's lap and goes to workbench. Stirs brush in bowl of water.*)

T: Well, I see that your time is up for today, Kathy.

C: O.K. (*Walks out of room with T and mother.*)

Discussion: January 17 Play Session

Kathy mentions the "bad man" in fear, at first, and then with anger. She tosses "him" into a pail of water, calls him stupid and naughty. Her anger spreads as she tosses a number of human and animal figures into the water and shouts, "Everybody's mean to me."

Kathy seems happier, not so anxious and tense, as she paints freely with the paints and clay. She speaks positively again of her father in the play situation.

She mentions her night fears and repeats· a number of times, "The cuckoo strikes at midnight." This is followed by direct anger expressed against her mother. She yells "I don't want my mommy to breathe. . . . If she doesn't stop, I'll dump her in there in the water and make her sweater get all wet." Frequently Kathy's fears and hostile feelings occur simultaneously. For Kathy, fear seems to motivate anger, and anger arouses fear.

Kathy reenacts the night fears over and over again, each time with less intensity, but as the session ends, Kathy, is still close to her mother.

JANUARY 24. PLAY SESSION WITH KATHY

C: (*Stands in doorway. Walks into room and goes to easel. Pushes brush around in water. Picks up truck and paints it with brush.*) Now I'm gonna paint with a different color. I want it to be black.

T: You want it to be black, hm?

C: Yes, I do. You know what I'm painting, Mommy?

M: What?

C: This color. Color the wheels. (*Puts the truck on floor and picks up a car.*) Those cars. I want to paint something else. I got another truck.

T: Mm-hm.

C: I'm gonna paint it another color.

T: You want everything to be different, hm?

C: No, not everything. Just some of them.

T: Oh.

C: Just some of the toys. This is real dirty. (*Paints tractor with brush. Drops tractor and runs back and forth across room.*) The clock struck midnight! The clock struck midnight!

T: The clock struck midnight, hm?

C: Oh, the cuckoo!

T: The cuckoo is coming, so you're running, hm?

C: I don't care. (*Handles nursing bottles. Pours water from small one into larger bottle and carries both to table.*) You gotta be very quiet when the cuckoo strikes midnight. Oh, the cuckoo struck midnight!

T: The cuckoo struck midnight again.

C: (*Dips paintbrush in large bottle and paints car.*) You know Donna?

T: Mm-hm.

C: You know, Donna was fighting a long time ago.

T: She did? You don't like her to fight with you, hm?

C: 'Cause she kicks me, then I kick her. She kicks me real hard, and I'll kick her real hard.

T: You don't like to be treated like that, do you?

C: No, I don't like that. (*Picks up another car and paints it with water.*) This is an automobile. Paint this a different color. (*Paints underside of car.*) Now this one isn't clean. Now this one. (*Pause.*) Walking on tiptoe!

T: You want to be quiet around here, don't you?

C: Yes. 'Cause the man on tiptoes is coming.

T: And are you afraid of the man?

C: Mr. Tiptoe is the tiptoe. Oh, look. Little dancing tiptoes! They're chasing me.

T: Do little dancing tiptoes chase you?

C: Yes. And they put me in the fire.

T: Oh, that's what you're afraid of. The fire.

C: (*Paints easel with water. Smiles at T. Puts fingers to mouth.*) Sssh, sssh, sssh.

T: We're going to have to be real quiet, hm?

C: Ssshh. (*Sits on mother's lap and speaks softly to her.*) You know what?

M: What?

C: Be very quiet. 'Cause when the cuckoo strikes midnight, she always plays the game.

M: Hasn't it stopped striking midnight yet?

C: No. When the cuckoo stops striking midnight, I'll fall asleep.

M: You'll fall asleep?

C: On your shoulder.

M: On my shoulder?

C: Yes, on your shoulder. Sssh.

T: You just want everything to be quiet while the cuckoo strikes, hm?

C: I said, "Be quiet." (*Dips paintbrush in water container on easel and paints door with water while sitting on mother's lap.*) I want to sit here.

M: You know, honey, I won't let anything hurt you.

T: Mommy wants you to know that she won't let anything hurt you.

M: You know that, don't you, honey?

C: I said, "Be quiet."

M: Why do we have to be quiet now for?

C: He's gonna hit me.

M: I won't let anything hurt you.

C: I think there's no real cuckoo.

M: You don't think there's a real cuckoo?

C: No. (*Points to male puppets on floor.*) Look at those silly things. Silly men.

T: Silly, silly men. That's what.

C: They wanta bite me.

T: You don't like those men because they'll bite you.

C: Yes. I'm gonna put them in fire.

T: You'll really fix them, won't you?

C: They'll be sorry, and they'll never come back again.

T: Mm-hm. Burn them right up.

C: Yes. And they can never come back again. (*Stands up and gets animal puppets.*) Not these puppets. These puppets are good to me.

T: They're the only good ones, hm?

C: Yes. 'Cause they have fur.

T: You like the fur ones.

C: Yes, I do. (*Again sits on mother's lap. Hums.*) Tickle me. Tickle me! (*Laughs.*) Tickle my hair.

M: Not now, honey.

C: Tickle my hair! Tickle my hair!

T: You want Mommy to tickle and tickle, hm?

M: You can tickle yourself.

C: No, you tickle me. Lift my hair up. Mommy, lift my hair up!

M: Honey, look. You just have a few minutes more, and I thought you would like to play down here instead of fooling around with Mommy.

C: I'm gonna stamp at you, Mom. (*Gets down from mother's lap and stamps her feet.*) I don't want to yell at Mommy. Mommy doesn't yell.

T: Doesn't your mommy yell at you?

C: No. Sometimes she does when I'm mean, and sometimes she doesn't.

T: Mm-hm. When you're mean, then Mommy yells at you.

C: Yes. She yells real loud. (*Handles puppet.*) Let's see inside the puppet. Inside the puppet. (*Peers inside the puppet.*) See in the puppet. This puppet.

T: You can look right down in there, can't you?

C: The cuckoo strikes midnight. I don't want to stay here now.

T: You don't have to stay, Kathy. You're the one who decides that. It's up to you. You can go whenever you want to go.

C: I want to go upstairs, Mommy.

M: You don't want to stay here any more?

C: No.

T: O.K., Kathy.

C: Leave these here. (*Puts puppets on the floor.*) What's in there? (*Points to mother's purse.*)

M: You know what's in there, honey.

C: What?

M: All my things.

C: Gum?

M: You're not getting any more gum today.

C: Is there gum in there?

M: No.

C: Let me smell.

M: No, I said, honey.

C: Let me smell something. I want to smell something.

M: No, honey.

C: I want to smell something.

T: Mommy just won't let you do it.

C: (*Hits mother and pulls at her skirt.*)

T: Mommy just won't let you do it.

M: Kathy. Are you having fun hitting me?

T: You just are angry, hm?

C: I'm gonna pull it off.

T: You'd like to pull it right off, hm?

C: I'm gonna pull her skirt.

T: You're really mad at Mommy.

C: I'm gonna tear her skirt.

M: Is that what you want to do?

C: Yes.

M: Kathy. Would you like me to pull you like that?

C: No.

M: Well, all right.

C: If you pull my socks down, if you hit me and kick me and kick me, then I'll hit you. I wanta look in your purse.

M: I'll let you look in my purse when we get in the car. I don't want you to take it apart now.

C: Smell it.

M: You can smell it and everything else later.

T: If Mommy doesn't let you do what you want to do, then you get angry.

C: Those silly guys. I'm gonna throw them in the fire, where they belong. (*Throws male puppets into pail of water.*) Going down the water drain. These silly things are going in.

T: All of them are going in. Just what they deserve.

C: And this dolly's going down the drain. There. (*Throws doll into pail after dropping diaper and pin into sandbox.*)

T: In she goes, too.

C: (*Picks up animal puppets.*) Do you think I should get these fur ones wet?

T: Do you suppose you should?

C: I don't know.

T: It's up to you, Kathy.

C: I don't want to put them in, but they got dirt.

T: You'd like to put them in, but yet you don't want to, because they have fur.

C: (*Places puppets to one side. Throws a small car into the pail.*) He's mean. And this little dolly's mean. Put them in the water.

T: So many mean ones.

C: Yes. So many, so many. The water's mean. (*Empties nursing bottles into pail.*)

T: Even the water is mean to you.

C: And the bottles are mean to me. (*Drops bottles into pail.*) And this water is mean to me. This is mean to me. (*Continues to throw toys into pail.*) Everything is mean to me. Everything is mean to me today.

T: Everything is mean to you.

C: Yes. This, and this.

T: And that's what they'll get when they're mean to you, hm?

C: They're all mean. This airplane's mean. Nothing is nice to me.

T: They're all mean to you.

C: Yes. Together with the bad wolf.

T: Together with the bad wolf, hm?

C: That bad wolf. (*Takes the paddle out of the canoe.*) I want to scoop with this for a delicious dinner. And scoop a delicious dinner. This isn't mean to me. This is a scoop for a delicious dinner.

T: And that's the only thing that's not mean to you hm?

C: Yes. Cooked a delicious dinner. (*Picks up bowl from pail of water and fills it with sand, using the paddle. Eats sand and spits it on floor. Makes faces.*) Pooh!

T: It doesn't taste good at all, hm?

C: You know what?

T: What?

C: You remember when Donna used to throw sand in my eyes?

T: Donna threw sand in your eyes?

C: Mm-hm. You remember Donna used to eat sand?

T: Donna used to, hm?

C: Yes.

T: And you want to do just what Donna does, is that it?

C: No! (*Eats sand with paddle. Spits on the floor.*) Pooh!

T: It really tastes bad, hm?

C: (*Continues to eat sand and make faces.*) Pooh!

T: It's pooey food.

C: Pooh! Pooh!

T: Kathy, you just have a few more minutes left to play today.

C: But I want to stay here. (*Eats more sand and spits on floor.*)
   I'm gonna stay here, and then I'll make bread and butter.

T: Then you'll make bread and butter?

C: Mm-hm. I just love bread and butter. I'm gonna spit down the
   water drain. (*Walks to drain and spits on floor. Peers down
   drain.*)

T: You're spitting right down there.

C: That's how the water comes.

T: Mm-hm.

C: (*Eats sand and handles paddle.*) I just got here, Mr. C. I just
   came here.

T: You just arrived right now.

C: I don't want to go home now.

T: You'd like to stay, hm? Well, there's just a couple minutes left.

C: But I don't feel like going home.

T: You feel like staying here?

C: Mm-hm. You know when I'm going to leave? Tomorrow.

T: You want to stay until tomorrow.

C: Yes. You know what doesn't bother me?

T: What doesn't bother you?

C: The chewing-gum sign. The one with the man. I'll empty my
   food all out. (*Throws bowl into pail after emptying sand
   into sandbox.*) There. Now. Good-by, Mr. C.

T: Good-by, Kathy.

Discussion: January 24 Play Session

Kathy begins the session by painting. Her attention span in the
playroom is longer, and she is more persistent in achieving her
goals. Her repetitive questions have disappeared, and she is more
independent of her mother.

Her fears appear again, but the feelings are much less intense.

Kathy's behavior is more like a game than an expression of deep or even real fear. She says, "I don't care" (about the cuckoo), and later, "When the cuckoo strikes midnight, she always plays the game." Kathy's mother accepts Kathy's strange actions, reassures her, "You know, honey, I won't let anything hurt you."

Kathy becomes hostile again, attacking the male puppets and throwing them into the "fire." She shouts, "I'm gonna stamp at you, Mom." Then, more sensitively, "I don't want to yell at Mommy. Mommy doesn't yell."

Kathy attacks "the silly guys" again and throws them into a pail of water. She throws the doll figures and some of the toys in the water, exclaiming, "Everything is mean to me today." Kathy also throws the "bad wolf" into the water too. Her fears are diminishing, both in nature and in intensity, in the playroom.

January 31. Play Session with Kathy

C: (*Runs to chair and pulls it in front of workbench. Puts clay on sheet of paper. Picks up male puppets.*) They're stupid.

T: Those are the stupid ones, hm?

C: Yes. And this is stupid. And this is stupid. (*Drops puppets into pail of water. Also throws a tractor and a diver figure into pail.*) They're all stupid today.

T: All of them are just stupid today.

C: They're going down the water drain.

T: They're going right down.

C: (*Picks up animal puppet and then drops it on the floor.*) I'm not even gonna talk to him. 'Cause he's not nice to me.

T: He isn't?

C: He didn't be nice to me today. He's the bad man.

T: And are you afraid of the bad man?

C: No. (*Throws toys from table on to floor.*) This is a stupid old car. This is a stupid old boat.

T: They're all stupid, hm?

C: Stupid old automobile. It's stupid. Do you know they're stupid?

T: Mm-hm. Every one of them just plain stupid.

C: Here's a cute little airplane. But this airplane is naughty, and you're gonna take it. Gonna throw it in the sand pile.

T: Throw it away, that's what.

C: And this is a little cutie.

T: Mm-hm.

C: That stupid shovel. (*Continues to throw toys on the floor.*)

T: You just feel like throwing them hard today, hm?

C: That's a stupid airplane, too.

T: I gather you don't like those stupid things.

C: N-O! (*Hits her mother.*)

T: You feel like hitting Mommy, hm?

C: I don't like you.

M: Why?

C: N-O!

T: You just don't like Mommy at all.

M: Do you want to tell Mommy why you're hitting her?

C: You know why?

M: Why?

T: Mommy just doesn't understand why you feel that way.

C: I'm gonna get some paint on you. (*Rubs paintbrush on mother's skirt.*)

T: That's what you'd like to do, hm? Paint Mommy all over.

M: Did you get mad at me for something, honey?

C: I'm hungry. That's why I'm hitting you.

M: You're hungry? You just had a sandwich and five cookies.

C: (*Continues to hit at mother's skirt with brush.*) You bad boy. You bad girl. I don't like you.

M: But I like you.

T: You just don't like Mommy.

M: You like to hit Mommy?

C: Where's that ball? Where's that bouncing ball?

T: Where could that have gone to?

C: Here's that bouncing ball. (*Picks up the red ball.*)

T: Mm-hm.

C: Where's that little tea? That little cup? That cup.

T: That little teacup?

C: Here it is. You know why I need it? I need it for something.

T: Mm-hm.

C: I'm gonna put it in this water. (*Drops cup into water container on easel. Dips brush into water and paints on paper and easel.*) I'm painting something.

T: You're painting just what you want.

C: (*Sighs. Continues to paint easel with water. One brush falls to the floor a few times.*) That stupid old paintbrush. That I don't like.

T: You don't like stupid things.

C: That stupid old paintbrush is always falling. I'll leave it there. (*Goes to workbench and pours water from nursing bottle over clay. Pours more water on clay and watches it trickle down bench to floor.*) For God's sakes!

T: It really splattered all over, hm?

C: God O mighty! Did you ever hear anything like that?

T: God all mighty?

C: Keep quiet! N-O, Mr. C.

T: O.K. That's the way you want it.

C: (*Throws animal puppet into pail of water.*) This one's been naughty, so I'll put him in a bath.

T: He's been naughty.

C: Everybody is naughty today.

T: Mm-hm.

C: I guess.

T: It sounds as though you aren't too sure about it.

C: (*Pokes in clay with paintbrush.*) Is that all today? Do I go home pretty soon?

T: Well, you still have about eight more minutes, Kathy.

C: O.K. But I just came here.

T: It seems as though you just came, hm?

C: Now I'm gonna make something else. (*Sighs.*) What I make now? (*Handles doll figures.*) What's in that big bag? Stuff, I guess. Gonna stand him up. (*Stands male doll upright.*) They're all stupid today.

T: Everybody is stupid

C: N-O. Don't talk about it. (*Walks back to workbench. Pokes brush into clay.*) I'm gonna make something else now. I changed my mind. I wanted to make a blueberry pie.

T: A blueberry pie?

C: Yep. And a blueberry cake.

T: Mm-hm.

C: (*Turns handle of vise with clay-covered hands.*) I'm getting this so dirty that you could hardly paint no more.

T: That's the way you want it to be, hm?

C: Yep. (*Walks to easel. Rubs brush over paper.*) Now I'm gonna paint something.

T: Just one more minute left, Kathy, and then you have to stop for today.

C: O.K. But first I gotta go wash my hands. I'm all through. Now I want to leave right now.

T: O.K. You want to leave now.

C: (*Walks out of the room with mother.*)

Discussion: January 31 Play Session

Kathy continues her direct hostile expressions toward the male puppets and "the bad man" and indicates that she is no longer afraid of "him." She hits her mother and says, "I don't like you," then tries to paint her.

Kathy's angry feelings toward her parents, in the play situation, are more direct and are also milder. She shows a great deal of positive feeling toward them and a constructive identification.

Kathy shows no fears in this session. She moves freely, is unconcerned about cleanliness, and paints spontaneously. She indicates in her frequent questions about remaining time that the play therapy experience may not have additional value for her.

FEBRUARY 6. TELEPHONE CONVERSATION WITH FATHER

F: I called you to see if there was anything you wanted to know.

T: Was there something particular you had in mind?

F: Everything is pretty doggone good. Of course, the fears don't all leave right away. They're diminishing, though. Her progress is really noticeable.

   By the way, I wanted to tell you one thing. One night on a television program a Mr. C was on, and someone said, "How do you do, Mr. C?" She turned to me and said "I know Mr. C."

She's a very good girl, and she's hanging less and less onto Dee.

February 14. Play Session with Kathy

C: (*Runs into room and picks up balloons.*) These are my favorite balloons.

T: You really like those, hm?

C: Yes. And this yellow one for you.

T: It's for me, hm?

C: No. The yellow one's for Mommy. This is her favorite balloon. There. Here, Mommy. (*Also hands T a balloon.*) Here for you. If I don't eat my supper, Daddy doesn't bring me any surprises. I just have to eat my supper. (*Looks at mother.*) Tell him about I don't eat my supper. O.K.? Tell him that.

T: You want Mommy to tell me about it?

M: You mean when Daddy says he's got a surprise, and you find out, and you don't want to eat, and you say you want your surprise right then? Daddy says you should eat your supper first, doesn't he?

C: Yeah. You tell him.

M: I did tell him.

C: Well, tell him now!

M: Again?

C: Yes.

M: Well, Kathy doesn't eat her supper, and Daddy comes home and has a surprise for her. And Daddy says, "Well, you can't have your surprise then, if you don't eat your supper."

T: But Kathy, you want your surprise right then and there, hm? And Daddy won't give it to you?

C: (*Walks to table with toys. Handles various items.*) This is an eggbeater. Got a bowl. And an eggbeater.

T: Mm-hm.

C: A hoe, too. (*Carries bowl to sandbox. Uses hoe to fill bowl with sand. Quietly plays with sand for a while.*) I want to tell you something. I can turn a somersault.

T: You can?

C: (*Starts to turn a somersault, then stops.*) I don't want to do one.

T: It's pretty hard on the floor, isn't it?

C: No, it's dirty, and I don't want to get my hair dirty.

T: Oh, I see. You don't like to get dirty, do you?

C: No. (*Carries bowl of sand to workbench. Hums. Presses clay with both hands.*) I need a rolling pin.

T: Well, that's very hard to work with, isn't it?

C: Yes. That's straining yourself.

T: It sure is.

C: Is my daddy new?

M: He's the only daddy you have.

T: You don't know whether he's new or not, hm?

C: He *is* new. (*Picks up a car and covers it with sand.*)

T: Kathy, you just have a short while longer left for today.

C: I still want to play here. O.K.?

T: You still want to play some more, hm?

C: Yes.

T: Well, you still have a little more time.

C: O.K., Mr. Clocky-pocky. (*Walks to dollhouse and handles some doll furniture. Also plays with small doll figure.*) The little baby sits down at her table. And here's her breakfast. Here's the stove. Little baby sits down at the table. Sit down at the table. (*Puts baby doll in small bed.*) Take a nap. Nap, 'cause it's time to. (*Sighs. Pours some sand into open refrigerator.*) Your dinner is ready on the table. I've got some in there. When your dinner is ready, you can come out of bed. I hear her hollering, "I want to come out of bed." I took her out. (*Picks up diaperless doll.*) Oh, this little baby wants to be fed, too. Do you know that?

T: Two little babies who want to eat.

C: Now, here, little baby. (*Feeds sand to both dolls, using the paintbrush for feeding.*)

T: You have just about time to feed them both a little bit, and then we'll have to stop for today, Kathy.

C: O.K. (*Feeds each doll a little more sand. Gets up and walks out of the room, followed by mother and T.*)

Discussion: February 14 Play Session

Kathy shows positive feelings toward her mother, giving her

the favorite balloon. She plays through the mealtime situation again, but with less intense feelings and reactions. She accepts the fact that unless she eats her dinner, there will be no surprises and does not confuse this rule with loss of love or status. She even asks her mother to describe the father's rule. Kathy sees her father in a slightly different way, wondering, at first, "Is my daddy new?" and then, "He *is* new."

February 21

On this day Kathy started to walk down to the playroom and suddenly stopped. She looked at the therapist and said, "I don't want to come here and play any more." "All right, Kathy," the therapist responded, "that's up to you." Kathy said, "N-O, N-O, N-O." She went up the steps, smiled, waved good-by to the therapist, and walked away with her mother.

May 15

About three months later, Mr. and Mrs. B came in for a brief talk with the therapist and reported the following:

F: We just came in to tell you that Kathy has just had her adenoids taken out.

M: Yes, and she was really wonderful. Some of the other children yelled and screamed and cried, but Kathy just went in quietly and went through the operation without a whimper.

F: When we told her we wouldn't be able to stay in the hospital with her, she just accepted it. She's a wonderful kid. We're very proud of her.

M: We told her we would be in to see her early in the morning, and then she could go home. When we took her to the hospital we sort of made a game out of it, and she joined right in.

F: We explained very simply what would happen while she was in the hospital, and she thought that would be fun.

Well, we don't want to take any more of your time. Kathy has been fine at home, just fine. She's been going to sleep without trouble and doesn't wake up at night, and there hasn't been any sign of her fears.

M: And she's doing everything she used to do, and she's so much happier. We're really grateful that she had the opportunity to come for play therapy and that we brought her here right at the beginning when the fears first started.

F: Well, we'd better go. Thanks again.

T: I've enjoyed working with you and Kathy very much. It's been a pleasure knowing you. So long.

M: Good-by and thank you, Mr. C.

EVALUATION OF KATHY'S PLAY THERAPY EXPERIENCES

Kathy's experiences in play therapy helped her to achieve a more realistic and acceptable relationship with her parents. She realized that they really did love her.

She expressed over and over again her anxieties, expressions of conflicts from within. Her struggle to suppress her hostility toward her parents aroused frustration and tension and contributed to her bizarre and marked fear reactions. The hostility itself was at least partially produced by the numerous family pressures on Kathy. Apparently Kathy interpreted the pressures to mean that her parents did not love her, or, more simply, that "they will love me only if I submit to them."

Kathy's anxiety was shown not only in her fears of people and animals but also in her terrific concerns over cleanliness and food, evidenced in the rituals of her play.

As Kathy felt secure in the relationship, as she felt accepted and respected by the therapist, she was able to bring out her hostile feelings. At first the angry feelings were indirect and subtle. In time, however, she focused them directly against her parents and expressed them repeatedly in a number of different ways.

Kathy's strange fears disappeared, and her anger was milder in intensity. Kathy relaxed in the playroom, played in a more concentrated way, and was no longer obsessed by a need for perfect cleanliness. She played freely and spontaneously with the sand, water, and paints.

At the same time the parents eased their pressures on Kathy, accepted her perceptions of people and things, attempted to understand her emotional behavior, and responded more frequently to her feelings.

The play therapy experience and the contributions of her parents in bringing about new family relationships helped Kathy to achieve more positive attitudes toward herself and others and to be more emotionally comfortable and free.

CHAPTER VII

Implications of Therapy outside the Playroom

Children grow emotionally in and through their relationships with other people. Study of these interpersonal relationships through play therapy sessions reveals that the effectiveness of any therapeutic relationship requires communication of faith, acceptance, and respect from the therapist to child. The detailed processes by which these attitudes are conveyed to children are at present largely unknown. There are some guides, though, to emotional growth that parents and teachers may use. There are some ways that may be helpful to parents and teachers in their attempts to help children with problems and confused emotions.

Some of the means to help children gain emotional insights are listening, conveying understanding, and providing opportunities for free emotional expression. Listening and conveying empathetic understanding are starting points in interpersonal relationships with children. They are active processes which complement each other. The listener is not only actively listening and empathizing, but he is at the same time conveying understanding through facial expressions and feeling tones.

Qualitative listening entails a particular type of response. It must include interest in, attention to, and concern for the individual child. It must exclude cutting children short, changing the subject, or in any other way denying children their feelings. The listener who really wants to help children grow emotionally has particular goals in mind. First of all, he wants to hear the feelings being expressed. He must hear the feelings in order to respond satisfactorily. He must hear the feelings in order to empathize, to feel along with children.

Listening to children's feelings is sometimes difficult. Feelings may be expressed with confusion or inconsistency, subtly, or perhaps ambivalently. It is the task of the listener, then, to reach the core of these feelings and to select the essence of the attitude. As he develops the listening attitude he may at first have to ask himself, "What feelings, what attitude is this child expressing to me now?" "What, essentially, is he telling me?" Eventually the listener should respond in a more spontaneous manner without first having to phrase questions in his mind. Sensitivity should become a natural part of the relationship, not an intellectual process.

The listener must indicate to the child his awareness of the feelings being expressed and his understanding of them. This may be accomplished implicitly at times, especially if the child realizes that the listener is empathetically following his feelings. At other times, particularly early in the relationship with the child, it may be necessary to show understanding directly through such expressions as "Mm-hm," "I see," or by paraphrasing the expressed feeling or attitude in a more succinct way, often prefixing it with "You feel," "I gather you feel," or "Is it that you feel?"

The person who has heard expressed feelings accurately and with empathy and has succeeded in conveying an understanding of them may see the child in a different way. The child, in turn, regards this type of listener differently. The child may feel that this person is interested in him as a person. In feeling understood and accepted, he may then want to reveal more of his inner feelings and attitudes to this warm, friendly person. Children who feel secure and comfortable in their relationships with adults are motivated to talk more and more about their real selves. They feel encouraged to explore more of their feelings and attitudes about themselves and others, and through this exploration they gain clearer, more realistic self-perception. In this process they may often condemn themselves and others and, in effect, create and recreate again and again the feelings and attitudes that are a part of their inner world. Children become wonderfully alive when they are listened to, understood, and accepted. They become freer and more expressive and during these times are more truly themselves, bringing out the highest qualities of their emotional natures.

Any interested person may become an empathetic listener and a valid communicator of emotional understanding. In assisting children to grow emotionally, listening, empathizing, and conveying understanding of feelings must be carried on regularly and consistently in a relationship. It is helpful to record chronologically, in some way, the feelings and attitudes expressed in a child-adult relationship of this type. These recordings may then be used as a way of seeing any modifications that have occurred in children's attitudes toward themselves and others. Children should never be forced or pressured in any way to express personal feelings. They will express their inner selves naturally and spontaneously when they feel secure enough in the presence of an adult who is empathetic and accepting.

Unstructured Media

Another way in which adults can help children to grow emotionally is by providing them with certain kinds of play materials. The best play materials are those which are not definitely structured, that is, which do not have clear shape or form. It is through these unstructured items, such as clay, finger paints, sand, and water that children can most easily express their feelings. Other media which are especially valuable include dolls and doll furniture, puppets, blocks, rubber knives and guns, scissors and paper, crayons, balloons, large comeback toys, and nursing bottles. These may be used by the child in spontaneous dramatic play, free association, and role playing.

Some children may use these media to express joy and happiness and good will, they may be used by others to work out hostilities and resentments. Jealousy, anxiety, and hatred may be projected onto these inanimate objects in an effort to release pent-up inner emotions.

Through his play the child may act out perceptions of himself, his family, and others that he would not dare reveal in his real world. These imaginary expressions themselves may enable him to live more securely in the world of reality. Children should be given time and a place with play materials to which they can go and where they can feel free to smear and mess, to draw and paint, to create and destroy, and sometimes to recreate themselves, their families, and other individuals.

While play itself frequently offers emotional release to children, it is not automatically accompanied by emotional insight. The presence of an adult whose aim is to help children clarify their feelings and accept them is an important requisite and hastens the process of emotional growth. The adult should permit the child to fully express his feelings through play materials and should encourage the child to use these materials in his own way. He should not be forced to play, however. The decision to play or not to play should be left to the child. Nor should he be pressured into using materials as others use them or as the world tells him he ought to use them. The materials have different meanings to different children, and their expressions should be unique. Play materials may represent families, friends, or attitudes or have a variety of other personal meanings. The child should be encouraged to pursue and explore his symbolic interpretations.

When a child asks, "How should I use this sand?" or "What shall I do with this sand?" the adult's attitude should be, "That's up to you; you can use it in any way that you want." This gives the child freedom to project his personal meanings onto the material. It also gives him the freedom to make decisions for himself. The inner process that a child experiences in making decisions and in personalizing his use of the material is in itself a growth process and, once achieved, will tend to make future problems and situations easier to handle emotionally.

From the above, a number of principles can be derived which adults may find useful in their contacts with children:

1. There should be some provision for a selected quantity and variety of play materials, both structured and unstructured, so that the child is free to select the type or quality of material he needs.

2. The child should be given ample opportunity to verbalize his emotions.

3. The adult should listen to the child's verbalizations, particularly to the feelings, and in some way indicate acceptance and understanding of them.

4. The child should decide whether or not he wishes to use the materials and whether or not he wishes to verbalize his feelings.

5. By his manner, reflection, expression, and tone the adult should show the child that he accepts his feelings as they are, neither criticizing nor approving but remaining totally acceptive.

6. Children should be permitted to express what they wish and not be obliged to follow a model or product that meets a social or art standard.

7. No attempt should be made to interpret to the child the symbolism involved in his play. Unless the adult makes the correct interpretation (an interpretation which coincides with the child's interpretation at that moment), the adult may generate disturbed feelings rather than aid the child in expressing them and working them through in his own way. The child's own judgment and expressed feelings provide the best clues to the meaning of the child's play, and these should be accepted exactly as they are.

People need not be psychotherapists; they need not know how to treat emotionally disturbed children in order to contribute to the emotional health of their children, their families, and their friends. The major requirements are strong motivations to understand human emotions and to accept these emotions as they are.

The Experiences of Mrs. A

The author once gave a talk to a small group of mothers, during which he presented some of the ways of understanding children's feelings and assisting them to grow emotionally. Mrs. A, one of the mothers present in the group, later made an appointment with the author. During the interview Mrs. A stated that she had never clearly understood Betty, her eight-year-old daughter. She said, "I have never really tried to understand her feelings, I guess.

Maybe it was because I was afraid of them. But now I want to try and help her to express her feelings more easily. I know she keeps so much to herself."

At the end of this conference, Mrs. A declared that she would make a real attempt to listen to Betty's feelings, to accept her feelings completely, and to indicate to Betty that she understood them. Approximately four months later Mrs. A reported the following:

"You won't believe it, but quite a bit has happened to me. When I left your office I was a very determined person, but I ran into all kinds of stumbling blocks. First of all, Betty wouldn't talk about her feelings. At least I could not detect or clearly follow her attitudes. Then one day I made a decision. I had been on the verge of carrying it out before and had thought about it a hundred times. I went to my parents' house. I told them I had something to say to them and I wanted to say it privately. I took them into the kitchen and closed all the doors and told them to sit down. I think it was the hardest thing I ever did. They looked at me in a puzzled way and wondered what in the world it was all about. After about two minutes' silence while I was struggling to hold onto myself, I finally said the words: 'I want you to know that there were many times in my life when I hated you both. I couldn't say it then, but you said many things to me and did many things to me which really hurt me, and I hated you for them.'

"Then I poured it all out to them, relating some of the incidents which had particularly affected me. To my amazement they listened, and they listened with understanding. They let me talk it out. You don't know how wonderful that made me feel. Then they told me that there were times when they hated me, too, and for the first time I was aware that I was listening to their feelings. When they were through talking, we all cried, and we knew that we really loved each other. For the first time in our lives, I believe, we could be thoroughly honest in expressing our feelings toward each other, and since then we have all been much happier people.

"After this incident I seemed to be a different person. I began to see many attitudes in Betty that I never knew existed before. I had never imagined that she was so compulsive about cleanliness, yet she had been telling me in so many ways for such a long time that she was afraid to get dirty. I wrote down some things that she had said to me each day for a few weeks, and there in my notes were her fears, holding her in, preventing her from being free and warm and friendly with other children. . . .

"So I bought some finger paints and plenty of paper, and I put a large table in the backyard. We sat down together, and I said to Betty, 'Now let's make the messiest picture we possibly can.' At first it was very difficult for her. She was reluctant. She was afraid to even touch the paints, and I didn't force her. It was difficult for me, too. I never imagined it would be so hard to smear paints. In a sense, we learned to do it together, and it released a lot of the feeling inside. . . .

"As time went on, Betty began to express some of her feelings more clearly. I encouraged her to go ahead and talk about them, even though sometimes what she said was somewhat critical of me and her father. It was hard to take, but I continued to accept her feelings nonetheless, and little by little I felt her feelings change. I felt my own feelings change, too.

"It was exciting to watch Betty become freer not only at home but also in the neighborhood. She became friends with some of the children on the block and invited them to the house. She played with her baby brother more and kissed him and showed him more affection. One day she set up a table in the yard, and they finger-painted together. This was the first time she had ever shown him much attention. . . .

"Her paintings changed, too. When the messy painting first started I thought it would last just a short time, and then for a while I wondered if it wouldn't continue forever. But it changed, and she began to make very beautiful designs and wonderful arrangements of form and color.

"Betty has shown improvement in many ways. She is much warmer and affectionate toward me. It's like having a new relationship with someone you've known a long time. We're more secure with each other. I'm not so critical of her any more. I just let her be herself. It's been a wonderful experience for me. We've grown together, and I know we'll continue to grow in this way. . . ."

Here is a mother who was able to utilize the child-centered philosophy, concepts, and guides in her family relationships. She was able in her own way to work out difficult emotional patterns with her parents and with her daughter. The process was not an easy one. It involved a strong emotional struggle and inner motivations which were maintained and strengthened even in the light of many threatening setbacks.

What happened to Mrs. A and Betty may be considered a normal growth experience which had been temporarily shut off by harbored fears and insecurities. As Mrs. A renewed her faith in herself as a competent mother, and as she accepted her attitudes toward her parents and respected her own judgments and values, she was able to free herself from inhibiting emotions. She was able to create a different kind of relationship with Betty. And in this warmth and inner peace, mother and daughter achieved understanding and acceptance of each other which enabled them to become happier and more creative in interpersonal relations.

Applications of Child-centered Play Therapy

1. AXLINE, VIRGINIA M. Entering the Child's World via Play Experiences. *Progres. Educ.*, 1950, 27(3), 68–75.
2. AXLINE, VIRGINIA M. Mental Deficiency—Symptom or Disease? *J. Consult. Psychol.*, 1949, 13(5), 313–327.
3. AXLINE, VIRGINIA M. Morale on the School Front. *J. Educ. Res.*, 37(7), 521–533.
4. AXLINE, VIRGINIA M. Nondirective Therapy for Poor Readers. *J. Consult. Psychol.*, 1947, 11(2), 61–69.
5. AXLINE, VIRGINIA M. *Play Therapy*. Boston: Houghton Mifflin Company, 1947.
6. AXLINE, VIRGINIA M. Play Therapy Experiences as Described by Child Participants. *J. Consult. Psychol.*, 1950, 14(1), 53–63.
7. BARUCH, DOROTHY. *New Ways in Discipline: You and Your Child Today*. New York: McGraw-Hill Book Company, Inc., 1949.
8. BILLS, ROBERT E. Nondirective Play Therapy with Retarded Readers. *J. Consult. Psychol.*, 1950, 14(2), 140–149.
9. BILLS, ROBERT E. Play Therapy with Well Adjusted Readers. *J. Consult. Psychol.*, 1950, 14(4), 246–249
10. COWEN, E. L., and W. M. CRUICKSHANK. Group Therapy with Physically Handicapped Children. II. Evaluation. *J. Educ. Psychol.*, 1948, 39, 281–297.
11. CRUICKSHANK, W. M., and E. L. COWEN. Group Therapy with Physi-

cally Handicapped Children. I. Report of Study. *J. Educ. Psychol.*, 1948, **39**(4), 193–215.

12. DORFMAN, ELAINE. Play Therapy Chap. 6, in *Client-centered Therapy*, by C. R. Rogers. Boston: Houghton Mifflin Company, 1951.

13. EISERER, P. E. Implications of Nondirective Counseling for Classroom Teaching. In *Growing Points in Educational Research*. Official Report. Washington, D.C.: American Educational Research Association, 1949.

14. FLEMING, LOUISE, and W. U. SNYDER. Social and Personal Changes Following Non-directive Group Play Therapy. *Amer. J. Orthopsychiat.*, 1947, **17**(1), 101–116.

15. LANDISBERG, SELMA, and W. U. SNYDER. Non-directive Play Therapy. *J. Clin. Psychol.*, 1946, **2**(3), 203–214.

16. MOUSTAKAS, C. E., and GRETA MAKOWSKY. Client-centered Therapy with Parents. *J. Consult. Psychol.*, 1952, **16**(5).

17. MOUSTAKAS, C. E. Situational Play Therapy with Normal Children. *J. Consult. Psychol.*, 1951, **15**(3), 225–230.

18. ROGERS, CARL R. *Client-centered Therapy*. Boston: Houghton Mifflin Company, 1951.

Index

215